"The Bible teaches that the Church is God's dwelling place, that among its members the blessings of the Kingdom of God can be experienced, and that God has given it the great privilege and responsibility of being Jesus Christ's instrument in spreading the Kingdom. It is only as we begin to realize this that the Church takes on real meaning for us."

In **When the Saints Go Marching Out,** Chuck and Anne Murphy help you find true meaning as a member of the Body of Christ. They show you what the Church really is, why it was created, and how it was meant to function. With this understanding, we can restore vitality to the Church by living the kind of lives we were meant to enjoy as God's adopted children.

The Murphys stress that it is God's plan for us to experience new life in Christ to the fullest, and to share this good news with others. You'll be challenged to commit your life to Jesus, to unite in fellowship with other believers, and to accept your role in the Church's ministry in and to the world.

When the Saints Go Marching Out

Chuck & Anne Murphy

Published by
√ chosen books

FLEMING H. REVELL COMPANY
OLD TAPPAN, NEW JERSEY

Scripture quotations, unless otherwise indicated, are from The Holy Bible, Revised Standard Version, © 1946, 1952 by Division of Christian Education of the National Council of the Churches of Christ in the United States of America.

Library of Congress Cataloging in Publication Data

Murphy, Chuck, 1922–
    When the saints go marching out.

    "A Chosen book"—T.p. verso.
    1. Church.   2. Church renewal.   3. Commitment to
the church.   I. Murphy, Anne, 1925–   .   II. Title.
BV600.2.M87   1987   262'.7   87-4525
ISBN 0-8007-9101-0

A Chosen Book
Copyright © 1986 by Chuck and Anne Murphy

Chosen Books are published by
Fleming H. Revell Company
Old Tappan, New Jersey
Printed in the United States of America

This book is dedicated to the saints we have known in churches in many places, who have responded to Christ's call to be His Body on earth and continue His ministry to the world. When those saints "go marching in" we are confident they will be greeted by, "Well done, thou good and faithful servants," because they were happy to go marching *out* to serve the One they call their Lord.

CONTENTS

When the Saints Go Marching Out

ONE

God's Creation

Many church members, both clergy and laity, are seeking to clarify their vision of the Church. They want to do this because they have rediscovered Christianity's claim that the Church is God's creation, not man's, and that its God-given mission and purpose offers an alternative to our man-centered existence.

The early Christians understood this clearly and eagerly responded to this "new thing" that God was about. They realized their own helplessness and knew that they needed a Savior in order to be free from the guilt, anxiety, fear, and despair of trying to be completely self-sufficient. Gratitude made it easy for them to allow Jesus to be their Lord and to open themselves to the guidance and empowerment of the Holy Spirit. They believed that they were called to be Christ's Body on earth.

In every generation there have been some who, like the first disciples, realize that the community of God's people is intended to be something unique, not just another institution that is not much better or worse than the rest of society's establishments. They understand that God called the Church into being for three reasons:

1. As a community in which He would dwell with His adopted children.

2. As visible evidence of the Kingdom of God on earth.

3. As His instrument for spreading the Kingdom in the world.

It has always been God's intention to have a community of believers in which He could be known and experienced. In the book of Exodus God promised that His people would be a kingdom of priests and a holy nation, and directed them to make a sanctuary that He might dwell in their midst (Exodus 19:6; 25:8). In the New Testament, Jesus promised those who love Him that He and the Father would come and make their home with them (John 14:23).

Jesus Christ was the fulfillment of these promises. He was the incarnation of the Word of God; He was the mind of God. Jesus was God enfleshed so that man could see first-hand the love and purpose of God. The Christian Church is called to be the incarnation of the risen, exalted Lord for a like reason: so that the love and purpose of God can be seen and experienced through and by flesh-and-blood people. Though shocking and incredulous to much of the world, one of Christianity's assured claims is that the Church has been given the power and authority to continue the ministry and mission of Jesus Christ.

The glorious message of the Christian Church has always been that of new life, beginning now through acceptance of Jesus as Lord and Savior, and continuing eternally. It is God's plan that His adopted children reach their highest potential and experience this new life to the fullest. Here is a story (author unknown) that offers insight into that plan.

The caterpillar is not the most attractive of God's creatures but it has potential: the potential to become a butterfly, which *is* one of the most attractive of God's creatures. Human beings are like caterpillars; often they are not too attractive. But even the least attractive of them, like the caterpillar, has potential. But—and here humans differ from the caterpillar—this potential is not automatically realized. It does not just happen that we become beautiful butterflies. There is no mysterious law of nature at work that spontaneously transforms us while we sleep unperturbed in a cocoon. It is entirely possible that we never become butterflies, but simply live out the days of our lives as caterpillars crawling along some twig never to know the joy and freedom of being a butterfly.

The business of providing the opportunity for caterpillars to become butterflies is perhaps one of the main jobs of the Church. Contrary to some belief, the Church is to assist in the birth of butterflies rather than somehow to make better caterpillars. Jesus' command to Lazarus' friends, "Unbind him, and let him go" (John 11:44), is a literal application of this principle. The Church members—both lay and clerical—are to be like midwives helping people give birth to their potential. The ministry of assisting at the birth of butterflies is far more rewarding than simply presiding at another convention of caterpillars. The Church is called to give evidence of a living, loving, powerful God who can be experienced, worshiped, and served by ordinary people in everyday life: One who can cause ordinary people to do extraordinary things.

God is never known in speculation about Him, but through encounters with Him. Although not limited to the Church such encounters are most likely to occur within the context of Christian fellowship. Exposure to the truths of the Christian faith and knowing how God acted in the past help people learn to recognize Him at work today in our lives.

God is known only as He reveals Himself to man and He does this in a variety of ways. Throughout history God has been known and experienced through covenants with His people. The Old Testament is concerned with the covenant of Law, which has provisions on both sides. In the first three verses of chapter twelve of Genesis, God directs Abram to leave his country and promises to bless him. Chapter seventeen of Genesis repeats this covenant: "I am God Almighty; walk before me, and be blameless. And I will make my covenant between me and you, and will multiply you exceedingly" (verses 1–2). The Old Covenant was codified in the Ten Commandments so that the people could clearly understand their part of the agreement; God would guide and protect His people as they obeyed the covenant. Unfortunately, knowledge of the Law does not give power to keep it. History demonstrates that man cannot, or will not, keep the covenant of Law.

The New Testament records how God entered human history as one of us in order to create a new covenant with His people. The outpouring of the Holy Spirit on the Feast of Pentecost, and the continuing outpouring of His Spirit, is the abiding seal and enabling power of this new covenant of grace. Jesus' life and ministry demonstrated that the covenant of Law and works could only be fulfilled by love—love of God and love of neighbor.

When Jesus called His first followers He taught them and commissioned them to proclaim the Good News, to witness to His life-changing power, to recruit others into the Kingdom under His Lordship, and to minister to people in His name and by the power of the Holy Spirit. The early Church became known as "the people of the way," and it is to that way that Jesus still calls us.

Down through the centuries the Church has allowed this call to become so altered that it often goes unrecognized. Consequently, the call to a new kind of life is seldom heard. Instead there is only a vague hope that the Church will somehow improve the quality of the old life. Moral leadership, help in solving problems, good advice, a temporary refuge from life, or gathering together with like-minded people are at best only some of the "fringe benefits" that the Church may offer. The Bible teaches that the Church is God's dwelling place, that among its members the blessings of the Kingdom of God can be experienced, and that God has given it the great privilege and responsibility of being Jesus Christ's instrument in spreading the Kingdom. It is only as we begin to realize this that the Church takes on its real meaning for us.

There are many ways of defining the Church. *The Book of Common Prayer* says it this way: "The Church is the community of the New Covenant, the Body of which Jesus Christ is the Head and of which all baptized persons are members. It is called the People of God, the New Israel, a holy nation, a royal priesthood, and the pillar and ground of truth."

Most Christian denominations agree that the Church is *one*, because it is one Body under one Head, our Lord Jesus Christ. It is *holy*, because the Holy Spirit dwells in it, consecrates its members, and guides them to do God's work. It is *catholic* (universal), because it proclaims the whole faith to all people, and *apostolic*, because it continues in the teaching and fellowship of the apostles, and is sent to carry out Christ's mission to all the world. The bottom line is that it is a community designed by God in which He can have a personal relationship with His people, and they can live the kind of life they were created to enjoy.

Once we understand what the Church is, who created it, and why it was created, we Christians can get on with the business of being the Church.

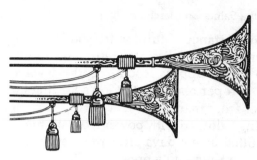

TWO

The Pattern
for the Church

God will never violate man's free will. If the Church is to evolve and fulfill God's plan for it, man must respond freely to God's initiative.

Foreshadowing the establishment of a community, God called Abram to leave his home and go to a new land with the promise to make of him a great nation. Yet Abram had to decide whether to go or stay. Later, God delivered the children of Israel from their bondage in Egypt, yet the decision to actually move out and follow Moses was one they had to make. After the Exodus, God directed Moses to receive offerings from the people for a sanctuary, "that I may dwell in their midst" (Exodus 25:8), but there was no coercion to give for this work. Each person could arrive at his own conclusion as to whether he believed that God really would dwell with man, and that a sanctuary was part of the plan.

In the New Testament, the Christian Church was born through a similar initiative and response. The book of Acts opens with Jesus' charge to the disciples to wait in Jerusalem for the promised baptism of the Holy Spirit. Would they wait or go out on their own? By this time the community had learned the importance of turning to God for guidance in making decisions, so the disciples returned to Jerusalem, settled into the Upper Room, and devoted themselves to prayer. (Proper response to God's leading inevitably evokes prayer from man.)

The promise of being "clothed with power from on high" (Luke 24:49) was fulfilled a few days after the Ascension, and gave evidence of the Kingdom's presence. The rushing wind, the tongues of fire, and the speaking in other tongues were physical manifestations of heavenly power in an earthly setting. That diverse group who met in the Upper Room on the Feast of Pentecost was bound and knit together by the Holy Spirit into a community of saints. Clearly, God was dwelling in the community He had established, was giving visible evidence of His presence and His Kingdom, and was using this small group of believers to bring others into the fellowship.

The continuing, vital work of the Spirit is to unite the members of the Body of Christ. The Church is not merely a collection of individuals, but a united, Spirit-filled fellowship. It is the Holy Spirit who makes this possible, not geographical closeness or mutual interests. A group thus united is able to participate in the risen Lord's life and continue His work on earth.

We see that as the Church grew, certain patterns, six in number, emerged in the believers' gatherings. Four of these are given in Acts 2:42: "And they devoted themselves to the apostles' teaching and fellowship, to the breaking of bread and the prayers."

Teaching was—and is—vital to the life of the Christian community. It is, first, the opportunity to educate the hearers in all that Jesus said and did. Second, without sound teaching, the community would wander into one of two extremes. Either it would become arid and eventually die, or move into sectarianism and heresy, the people of God becoming fanatics who unwittingly harm the cause of Christ. The tremendous power that is released to the Church by the Holy Spirit has been compared to a truckload of wet concrete. If the concrete is poured into molds, it can become the foundation for a cathedral, or a wall for protection, or any number of useful things. If it is simply dumped out, it ruins the ground and serves no good purpose. Sound teaching provides molds that allow the power that the Spirit gives people to be properly channeled. This enables the experience of the empowerment by the Spirit to produce spiritual fruit rather than religious nuts.

Fellowship is listed as the second mark or pattern of the early Church. The community in which God would dwell must not only be in fellowship with Him, but must live in a new kind of fellowship with each other. If these people are to be visible evidence of the Kingdom of God on earth, and are to be used as God's instrument for spreading His Kingdom in the world, they have to demonstrate a love and power in their lives together.

The Christian fellowship that the New Testament speaks of is not what most of us today know as fellowship. It was not a social activity in a Fellowship Hall through the planning of a Fellowship Committee. Rather, it was experienced whenever two or three met together as a corporate family and shared what God was doing among and with them. It is a sad commentary that fifty-three percent of the people who are baptized each year drift away from the Church. These people have not participated in the Christian community by sharing their lives with others.

Christian fellowship is a sacrament in which God communicates His grace through human channels. He moves, acts, teaches, guides, and builds up His Body through members of the Body. God feeds the Church in the give and take of Christian fellowship and in the power of the Holy Spirit. The time together should leave us with the clear knowledge that we have been channels of the Spirit, and have fed others as we ourselves have been fed.

Paul wrote to the church in Rome that he longed to be with the members "that we may be mutually encouraged by each other's faith, both yours and mine" (Romans 1:12). Those who minister to each other and share their lives within the Body of Christ do not drift away. They become more deeply involved in the life, work, and worship of the Church, and grow spiritually by leaps and bounds.

The author of the letter to the Hebrews wrote, "Let us consider how to stir up one another to love and good works, not neglecting to meet together, as is the habit of some, but encouraging one another, and all the more as you see the Day drawing near" (Hebrews 10:24–25). True Christian fellowship supplies the support and encouragement that are needed in order to live as faithful Christians in the secular world. It is the Body of Christ, rather than the individual Christian, that is the instrument through which God's plan for the world will be accomplished.

The breaking of bread, which is listed as a pattern of the early Church, probably meant both the sacramental meal that Jesus instituted at the Last Supper, and a kind of "covered dish supper" that the Christian fellowship shared. Both of these are means of feeding and strengthening the community of believers, and both are needed today, just as they were in the first century.

Prayer is the fourth pattern listed in Acts 2:42. The early Church was a praying church because it is recognized that prayer and ministry must be inseparable. Jesus had shown them this in His own ministry, and they were conscientious to follow His example. Their prayers undergirded their ministry. "Lord, stretch forth Thy hand to heal" and "Grant to Thy servants to speak Thy word with all boldness" were the foundation for the miracles and proclamation of the early Church, and built the early Christians' fervor for a fifth pattern: *evangelism.*

The zeal and enthusiasm of the first Christians came from three sources:

1. They knew Jesus in a personal way, and recognized Him as Messiah, Savior, and Lord.
2. They were filled and empowered by the Holy Spirit. This was not a onetime event of Pentecost, but a continuing receiving and empowering.
3. They had a vision and a purpose. They were convinced that God had called them to proclaim the Good News of redemption, and that He would be with them in this work.

I would like to emphasize the fact that God never asks anyone to do anything without giving him or her the power for the task. He empowers people today as surely as He did in the early Church. Neither has the Great Commission changed. "Go therefore and make disciples of all nations, baptizing them in the name of the Father and of the Son and of the Holy Spirit, teaching them to observe all that I have commanded you; and lo, I am with you always, to the close of the age" (Matthew 28:19–20).

Evangelism continues to be a combination of personal witnessing and sound teaching and preaching, always pointing to Jesus as Lord and Savior. It is the work of the whole Church and not just those who are "professional Christians." Peter's advice is for all of us: "Always be prepared to make a defense to any one who calls you to account for the hope that is in you, yet do it with gentleness and reverence" (1 Peter 3:15). When we know whom we serve and what we believe, people will seek us out, and if we witness to them with gentleness and reverence we can be assured that God will honor our efforts. Overzealousness and lack of common sense can turn people off to our efforts to witness and evangelize.

Jesus wants His followers to be "fishers of men," but a good fisherman knows that not all fish will respond to the same bait. Dean Robert B. Hall, an Episcopalian evangelist, tells about a man who once fell down a deep well, and although there was not enough water in it to drown him, he was unable to get out. During his dark, damp ordeal he yelled himself hoarse in an effort to attract a rescuer. Finally, when no help came, he decided in desperation to try prayer. To his amazement, he discovered as he prayed that he became filled with peace and even joy. He felt that God was truly with him. He called out again for help, and this time someone heard him, threw him a rope, and pulled him to safety. The man was so delighted that he had "found God" during his stay in the well that he devoted the remainder of his life trying to push people down wells! It is comforting to know that we are not required to push other people down our particular "well" in order to witness.

In conjunction with the witness of individual Christians there remains the Church's need to witness from the pulpit to the life-changing power of Jesus Christ, to teach the biblical truths, and to proclaim with conviction the Christian faith. Helmut Thielicke in *The Hidden Question of God* states: "Whether a church is living or dead depends exclusively on its proclamation. If someone can show that the church is not a preaching church, and if he can also show that it is not made up of a community which responds to its message in prayer, hymn, and act, then he is describing a corpse."

Failure to teach the Bible and proclaim the faith is one of the greatest weaknesses I see in many mainline branches of the Church today. I have heard pronouncements by certain leaders that reflect an appalling lack of both knowledge and faith. If those elected or appointed to leadership within the Church display such abysmal ignorance of the Bible and faith of the Church, which inevitably results in their own lack of faith, it is little wonder that there is in many places a paucity of mature faith within the Church.

Dr. Thielicke says of this, "Ignorance of what the Christian faith is all about is horrendous today. . . . The primary need, then, is for instruction and information. Even practicing Christians need this, partly because they are confused and partly because they are too ignorant at some points. . . . Those who are not conversant with the foundations of their faith cannot be mature Christians. . . . Either the Church will do its basic work (imparting the central contents of the Gospel to practicing Christians, marginal members, and those who are completely outside) and turn to the foundations of its faith, or it will die."

This gives a fresh urgency to Jesus' command, "Feed My sheep." Even when some preachers or theologians do attempt to teach they fall into the trap of being too erudite. Living out Christianity is not always easy, but I do not believe it is all that hard to understand. Just as there are people who can complicate simple instructions, there are preachers, seminary professors, and theologians who complicate Christianity. Talking over a congregation's head only produces wandering attention. They seem to forget that Jesus said, "Feed My sheep," not "Feed My giraffes"!

A sixth and critical pattern of the Church's mission is to *nurture* its members. Nurture is defined as both feeding and education or training. Feeding Christ's sheep demands that Christian education be a lifetime process of aiding people to know Christ and make Him known; in other words, to worship Jesus as Lord and Savior, and in turn to serve others in His name.

Worship has always been a vital and visible function of the Christian Church. It is the expression of the worth-ship of God, and should call forth the deepest feelings of the worshiper. Here the Psalms are among the richest guides to worship. They imply that proper worship of God is a total

23

offering of self. This involves songs of praise, prayers of thanksgiving, and involvement of body, mind, and spirit. They suggest a joyful abandonment of self as the worshiper is caught up in awe and wonder at the greatness and goodness of God.

In the pattern of nurture in the Church, worship and service go hand-in-hand. Meeting both physical and spiritual needs is involved in service. Paul Tillich once said, "Religion is first an open hand to receive a gift and second an acting hand to distribute gifts." Christian discipleship is a matter of both giving and receiving.

On the night of the Last Supper, Jesus instituted two sacraments. The first was that of bread and wine, the second of towel and basin. When Jesus washed the feet of His disciples, in the role of servant, He tied together the worship of the Church and the service of the Church. Worship without service is only pious ritual and ceremony. Service without worship is merely humanism. The Church must never forget the example of the One it calls Lord, whose ministry set the pattern for the Church.

Jesus was totally committed to His mission and ministry, and His followers must also be committed. We must accept our ministry of representing Christ, of bearing witness about Him wherever we may be, and according to our God-given gifts and talents, of continuing His mission and ministry in and to the world. This is a great privilege and responsibility. By following these patterns established for us in the early Church we can begin to fulfill a great call. But we must remember that the foundation for it all, the place we must start, is with a commitment to Jesus as our personal Lord and Savior.

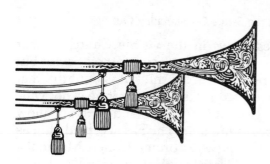

THREE

The Need
for Commitment
to Jesus

Jesus continues to work, as He did with the first Christians, through those who belong to Him and are committed to Him. Commitment means to pledge or consign your will to another's. We become serious about our status as Christians when we give our lives to Jesus Christ in trust that He is who the Bible says He is: the Son of God and Savior of the world. This is the first commitment a Christian makes. We pledge, or bind, ourselves to a certain course of trying to follow Him as the Lord, the "Boss" of our lives. That states it simply, but it is not a simple thing to do.

It is important to understand that Christian commitment is like signing our names to a contract and letting God fill in the blanks. We are more apt to do this if we believe that when we take this step, God will accept us, will manifest Himself to us in ways we can see and understand, and will honor our efforts to follow Him. It is the desire for a higher quality of life that motivates a person to take this leap of faith. Dissatisfaction with the status quo is usually what triggers the desire for change.

One of the greatest flaws in the visible Church is that many of its members want to claim Jesus as their Savior but do not want Him to be their Lord. I think it is doubtful that a person has really accepted Jesus as Savior if he is not willing for Him to be his Lord. It is certain that he will not allow Him to be the Lord of his life unless he has accepted Him as his Savior. Perhaps this is why former United Methodist Bishop Raines of Indiana described the Church as "a glob of people continuing a job they never seriously began."

In our first book, *There's No Business Like God's Business,* I said that most people have to get kicked into heaven. I now am convinced that *everyone* has to get kicked into a relationship with God, although He would rather "kiss us into heaven." There are varying degrees of kicks, but everyone has to experience some kind of pain—physical, mental, or spiritual—before he or she will turn to Jesus as his or her Savior. It may only take the form of a deep dissatisfaction with life, a sort of "divine discontent," to bring us to this point. No one will accept a Savior until he knows he needs one. We self-centered, arrogant people have to be brought to our knees before we will look up to God. Even the nominal Christian must reach this point.

I read of a family of wayward church members: a father and two sons, John and Sam. After many years of active membership they had grown cold and indifferent. The minister and other church members visited regularly urging them to turn from their backslidden condition, to come back to worship and involvement in parish life. None of the efforts seemed to impress the family.

One day while he was working in the pasture John was bitten by a rattlesnake. He was rushed to the doctor, and after doing all he knew to do, the doctor told the family: "It's up to God now. All you can do is pray." The father went to the minister's house and asked him to pray for John's recovery. This is the prayer that the minister is reported to have prayed: "O wise and righteous Father, we thank Thee, for Thou hast, in Thy wisdom, sent this rattlesnake to bite John in order to bring him to his senses. Father, this is the first time he has felt the need for prayer in years. Please let this experience lead him to genuine repentance. And now, Father, wilt Thou send another snake to bite Sam, and a big one to bite the old man. O God, this family understands rattlesnakes, so Lord, send bigger and better rattlesnakes. Amen."

Many nominal Christians are like that family. Of course God does not send rattlesnakes to bite people, but adversities are useful in getting some people's attention. A lot of folks do not understand grace, but they do understand adversity, trouble, and problems. They will not respond to grace, but they will to trouble. It is better to have life kick you into the Kingdom than never to come in at all.

Once we make a serious commitment to Jesus our goal for the rest of our lives is to find ways to translate this into a daily living pattern. If I am going to turn my life over to the Lordship of Christ it means that I will deliberately allow Him to influence my decisions and behavior in my activities and relationships. God knows this is not going to be easy! I need all the help I can get. The primary source of this help comes from opening myself to the Holy Spirit for guidance and strength. A secondary source of help comes from the words and examples from Scripture.

The Gospels show that Jesus met people where they were. When He performed His first miracle—turning water into wine at a wedding in Cana—He died to self and ministered to His mother and the other wedding guests. His words to His mother, "Woman, what does your concern have to do with Me? My hour has not yet come" (John 2:4, NKJV), indicate that this was not a time Jesus would have chosen to manifest miraculous power. Yet, because of His mother's request, and her obvious concern for the success of the wedding festivities, Jesus complied, and met the need at hand.

This incident has helped me to see how to let Jesus be the Lord of my life in some practical ways. When the children were young and I had work to do around the house I may have felt that "the hour had not yet come" to stop what I was doing if a child wanted to hear a story, or later, when a teenager needed to talk over a problem. If I let the need override the household schedule by laying aside my immediate plans, I had an opportunity to let Jesus be Lord. This turned a frustrating interruption into a chance to acknowledge Jesus as Lord by obeying His command to love, and as Savior by preventing me from feeling like a self-righteous martyr. Such small examples have blessed and enriched my life, and helped produce a rich harvest of family love.

We discover that at some time after our initial commitment to Christ, the Holy Spirit begins a housecleaning job on us. This may be expressed as conviction of sin, which is another way of acknowledging that some changes need to be made. It may simply be noticed as a reordering of interests and priorities. In either case, we realize that although Jesus accepts us as we are, He doesn't encourage us to remain in that state. This process of being molded into the image of Christ is sanctification, and it is a lifetime process. Sanctification does not take place against our will, but only through our response to the Holy Spirit.

Jesus was God's idea of perfect man, but to understand this it is helpful to remember what Jesus meant when He said, "Be ye perfect." To be perfect is to be what we were created to be. A chair can be said to be perfect if it does not wobble, and people can sit on it; it does what it was created to do. Jesus was perfect because He did what He was begotten to do. The command to be perfect is not a demand that we never make a mistake, or that we be absolutely morally pure. It does not even demand that we are to reach some vague state of perfection in our own strength. It is a command that we be what we were created to be and, as I said earlier, God never asks a person to do anything without giving him the power to do it.

I begin this process of being perfected when I commit my life to Jesus as my Savior and my Lord, and then allow the Holy Spirit to change me—to mold me—into what I have been reborn to be. This is what Christ has called each of us to do. He only asks us to be open and obedient. The Holy Spirit is the One who will perfect us, if we will allow Him to do so.

If we are to cooperate with the Holy Spirit in His work in and on us, two things are required: submission and discipline. Neither comes easy, which may be why Jesus warned His followers to count the cost. He insisted that they understand that following Him is not to be entered into lightly.

All too often we want Jesus to follow us and be there to help when we need Him, but that is not the way it works. We are not called to serve Jesus in an advisory capacity. He is not a life jacket or a protection policy for a follower who insists on being in charge. He did not promise to follow us, but demanded that we follow Him. His presence is for the purpose of directing and empowering us in His work and in our living the Christian life. This is something that the nominal Christian, the casual Christian, the in-name-only Christian does not understand. The kind of commitment that Jesus expects from His followers is something that the casual Christian does not offer Him, and has to do with submission and discipline.

The word *submission* has unpleasant connotations because the thought of surrendering, living in obedience or resignation, is not inviting. It sounds lifeless, conquered. For many people submission sounds like life under a dictatorship or life as a doormat.

St. Paul gave a very different understanding of submission in Ephesians 5:21: "Be subject to one another out of reverence for Christ." This describes a way of life that enables Christians to live together in peace and harmony, respecting and affirming one another. It requires truth and grace in both our listening and speaking. Involvement with others and commitment to Christ become the glue that holds the fellowship together.

Personal commitment to Jesus that does not lead to involvement with other members of His Body is a self-centered religion that is completely foreign to what Christ established. Jesus did not come to establish a bunch of "me and God" units. He came to create a community, a fellowship, a family. I believe that God knows nothing of solitary religion. The uninvolved Christian wants Christ and His Church to be there when needed, but does not want Christianity to interfere with his desire to be in control of his life.

Once I was asked to conduct the funeral of a man who many years earlier had been somewhat active in my parish. It was a graveside service, and when I arrived there was only a handful of people present—none of whom I knew. When the hearse arrived, a young man came over and introduced himself as the man's son. After the service, a young lady introduced herself as the man's daughter and said, "Daddy just loved this parish. He went to church every chance he got." Daddy had been to church only once in the seven years I had been there. Then she added, "I love this parish also, but I haven't attended as often as I would have liked." I am sure that she had not been there once during those seven years. I didn't answer her. I just looked at her. Were her remarks due to embarrassment or guilt? Surely she knew that she was not fooling God. Did she think she was fooling me? How do you reach families like that one? How do you get them committed to Jesus to the extent that they will get involved in the life, worship, and work of the Church? People like that are harder to reach for Christ than those who are actually hostile to Him. Hostility often is due to the person being under conviction by God.

Discipline is vital to effective Christian discipleship. It is the training that develops self-control and enables us to grow into mature Christians. Discipline allows us to develop a prayer life and to study and understand Scripture. Through discipline we learn to avail ourselves of study courses and conferences that increase our knowledge and understanding of Christianity. Proverbs 12:1 reminds us that whoever loves discipline loves knowledge. Hebrews 12:11 promises that although discipline may appear painful for a moment, it brings "the peaceful fruit of righteousness to those who have been trained by it."

Secular vocations recognize that discipline is necessary in order to attain success. Recreational sports such as jogging, tennis, swimming, racquetball demand discipline. Everything in life that is worthwhile requires discipline, so it should not surprise us that full-time Christian discipleship also calls for discipline.

Discipline and *disciple* come from the same root word, and a look at their definitions helps us understand why discipline is always a part of effective discipleship. The *American Heritage Dictionary* defines disciple as "a person who subscribes to the teachings of a master and assists in spreading them," and discipline as "training that is expected to produce a specified character or pattern of behavior." In light of these definitions it is easy to see why our Lord urges, "Take my yoke upon you, and learn from me . . ." (Matthew 11:29). Whenever anyone really subscribes to the teachings of a master and wants to assist in spreading such teachings, there comes an obligation to submit to the training necessary to produce a specified character or pattern of behavior. When applied to Christians, the Church labels this process sanctification. This never takes place without our consent, however, and we cannot or will not give this consent without first making a lifelong commitment to Jesus.

This foundation is crucial. We cannot grow spiritually or find the help and assurance Jesus has for us or live "perfect" lives without committing ourselves to Him. But we must not stop there. To follow Jesus means that we have a further commitment to make: to His Church and to its members.

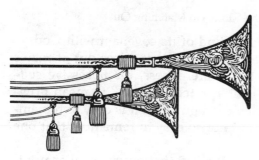

The Need
for Commitment
to the Church

Commitment to the Church means that we believe God has a plan for the world, and that the Church is His instrument for implementing that plan. The Church, and Christianity itself, is more than a collection of individuals who have made a commitment of their lives to Jesus Christ. It is a fellowship with a mission, a corporate body in covenant with God.

God still loves the world He created—in spite of its rebellion against Him. The Old Testament and the New are records of God taking the initiative to bring the world back into the love relationship with Himself that He originally intended.

We see God's plan for reconciliation begin when He chose the Israelites to be His instrument of salvation for the world. He made a covenant with Israel through Abraham and gave His promises and requirements. Israel, in turn, pledged loyalty and obedience. The call of Israel was to be "the servant Israel" who would glorify God among all of the nations of the earth. Israel's history is an interpretation of

33

s against the background of its covenant with God.

With any call comes the danger that arises out of man's inordinate pride, his self-centeredness, his obsessive self-love. The Israelites misinterpreted "chosen" to mean privileged, instead of selected for a purpose. It is easy to remember that one is called, but not so easy to remember that one is sent.

It is also easy to ignore the fact that every peculiar privilege that God bestows carries with it some peculiar responsibility. When the idea of Israel as "God's pet" prevailed, the result was inevitable. Drunk with pride and self-esteem, the nation made light of God's demands. Her great sin was her disloyalty to God and His covenant. The prophets convicted the people of their sin, so they stoned the prophets. People sought escape through ceremony and ritual, rather than obedience. As they ignored their role as God's instrument of salvation—that they be "a light unto the Gentiles"—their religion became one of legalism. Their emphasis was on the letter of the Law instead of its spirit as they wrapped their religion around themselves as a means of preserving their uniqueness.

In spite of their stiff-necked disobedience, God's plan was not thwarted. Salvation would still come through the Jews. God had chosen them to be His instrument, and even though it finally narrowed down to one Jew—one Man who put obedience to God ahead of everything else—salvation was put into effect. Jesus, representing the Jewish people, became the salvation for all mankind. God remained faithful to His promise! We have all heard the phrase, "How odd of God to choose the Jews," but He is a God of particularity. One people was chosen from among all people. One Man's death would effect justification for all, and one territory was designated as the arena for the greatest event of all time.

Jesus was born a Jew of the tribe and lineage of David. He was educated in Jewish Law and custom, and regarded

Himself as a true, loyal Israelite. He wanted to restore to His people a sense of the meaning of Israel's call, and considered Himself as "The Restorer" of that call. If Israel could be recalled to a true sense of her mission, God would stretch forth His hands to heal and save through them. Before He died, Jesus took great pains to implant His mind and message in a specially chosen circle of people who believed that He was the long-awaited Messiah. Gradually they came to see that they were corporately "The True Israel." The early Church did not think of itself as a new community in the world, but as the old true people of God radically renewed. Christ had instituted a new covenant between them and God, a covenant of grace instead of Law.

This band of loyal followers was made the mystical "Body of the Messiah" in such a way that when they went forth into the world on their mission and ministry, they did so with the power and authority of Christ Himself. Jesus transformed the Church from a nation into a divine organism that was the incarnation of its risen, exalted Lord. What they did was done in His power and in His name. Unfortunately, this concept has been lost in much of the New Israel, the Church today. Nevertheless, the authority and the power are still there, waiting for believers to step out in faith and act in His name.

I believe that it is imperative that Christians know and understand that they are members of this New Covenant with God. It is a covenant that includes great privileges and heavy responsibilities. We must be aware that it will take a united effort if we are to fulfill our God-given task. Although commitment to Jesus is the first step, it is still only the first step. The second step is commitment to the Church of the New Covenant. This, for many people, is more difficult than either personal commitment to Jesus or commitment to the other members of their local parish.

Somehow "the Church" sounds vague and impersonal to

many Christians. It is difficult to "plug in" on a personal note, yet unless we do, we will never be able to broaden our vision and see beyond the boundaries of self or local parish. Both "Lone Ranger" Christians and parochialism are a hindrance to the Church's work in the world.

Because we hesitate to commit ourselves to something unfamiliar, it is important to learn about the programs, disciplines, and functions of the denomination or fellowship to which we belong. We need to understand its overall goals and the means it uses to attain them. We must also understand the biblical teachings about the Church and its purpose, for if we have strayed from these teachings, we are obliged to pray and work for a return to them.

In both the Old Testament and the New we find that God calls His people together as a body of believers, and works in and through them in spite of their imperfections. It is comforting to remember this as we may struggle to come to terms with things that our particular denomination may, or may not, do in ordering its national life. To be committed to the Church in this sense means believing in the sacred nature of God's call to His people, and believing in the stated mission of the Church—despite mistakes and shortcomings. It means agreeing with St. Paul when he asserts that God has put all things under Christ's feet, and has made Him the head over all things *for the Church*, which is His Body (Ephesians 1:22–23). This can become personal for us as we give assent to the doctrines and disciplines of the denomination of our choice, and support its programs and missions with our prayers, our time, talent, and money. In every denomination the individual Christian can pray, "Lord, revive Thy Church, beginning with me." We can also vow to pray, work, and give for the extension of God's Kingdom on earth, believing that He is able to perfect the Church as a whole, and each of us who belongs to it.

I have absolute trust that anything done to God's glory, or

according to His will, will be honored by God. If it is right, He will bless it, and if it is wrong, He will redeem it. This takes a lot of the anxiety out of both living and trying to serve our Lord. Church history vividly reveals that not everything done by the Church has been an attempt to be in His will or to give glory to Him. We Christians must be careful to seek God's will in what we do, and be zealous that it give glory to Him.

The Christian life is one of activity. One cannot stand still in the Christian life. Like riding a bicycle, we are either going forward spiritually or we are falling off. Christ has called us to be members of His Church and active participants in its mission and ministry. Throughout history God has been saying to the people He has called: "Don't just stand there, do something!" God will not guide us until we move forward in obedience to His orders. I am convinced that the Red Sea did not part until the first Israelite put his foot in the water. The Church and its individual members, like Jesus Himself, are "under orders."

Long ago, Joshua said to Israel: "Now therefore fear the Lord, and serve him in sincerity and in faithfulness; put away the gods which your fathers served beyond the River, and in Egypt, and serve the Lord. And if you be unwilling to serve the Lord, choose this day whom you will serve . . . but as for me and my house, we will serve the Lord" (Joshua 24:14–15). He was saying, "Make a decision, then serve the choice you have made." Centuries later, John the Baptist said to the Jews, "Repent, for the kingdom of heaven is at hand. . . . Bear fruit that befits repentance, and do not . . ." stand so arrogantly upon your status as children of Abraham (Matthew 3:2, 8–9). John was saying that there is more to being God's people than just being a member of the Old Covenant. The same is true about members of the New Covenant. Lives must confirm what lips profess as faith.

John Henry Newman, theologian and church leader of the

late 19th century, said that the turning point in his life came when he remembered what God expected of him. He said, "God created me to do Him some service. He has committed to me some work which He has not committed to anyone else. I have a mission." This is the same thing the disciples discovered after Christ's death and resurrection. It is a discovery all Christians must make. We need to become aware that we are important to God, and that our lives count. The future of the Church is in our hands.

Christians are called to worship God, serve Christ, and live a totally new kind of life in a fellowship of love, joy, peace, and power. We are a new creation—holy, set apart—to manifest and prepare the way for the Kingdom on earth. The standards, values, goals, and tasks of Christians are different from those of non-Christians. St. Paul once said to the Corinthian Christians, "Are you not . . . behaving like ordinary [people]?" (1 Corinthians 3:3). He could think of nothing worse to call them. Christians are not ordinary people. We are a third race, neither Jew nor Gentile, but a new creation. We cannot afford to settle for the lowest common denominator. It is Satan's aim to get Christians to think and act like ordinary people.

Christian commitment is best expressed in the local church through its life, work, worship, and commitment to the other members. It is in the local parish that we find we are living out our commitment to Jesus. This simple statement is both the good news and the bad news of church life today. It is good news for those fortunate enough to belong to churches where Jesus is proclaimed as Lord, and acknowledged as Head of the Church. In a parish where the Bible is studied, taught, and learned, where the gifts and power of the Holy Spirit are accepted and employed, and where the members of the church have accepted the commission Christ gave to His Church, you will find visible evidence of the Kingdom of God on earth. In such an environment, the spiritual life of the individual can grow and flourish, and the original commitment to Jesus that brought us into the Church will increase and bear fruit.

It is bad news for those who belong to parishes where one or more of these elements are missing. A parish may be active in many endeavors, but if Jesus is not allowed to be the Head, with the commission He has given His Church its primary concern, nothing much of a lasting nature is accomplished. Such parishes are like a chicken that has just had its head chopped off. They still flop around with great activity and commotion, but are dead just the same. Mere activity does not denote life. It is terribly difficult to maintain an original commitment to Jesus and to reflect the joy, peace, and power He offers in that kind of parish. It is possibly a slight exaggeration, but I have heard it quoted that if God removed the Holy Spirit from the Church today, ninety-five percent of what goes on would continue. That is because much of the activity has nothing to do with the real purpose of the Church.

The second chapter of the book of Acts mirrors what a church should be. It describes a community where the power and love of God were experienced and manifested in an atmosphere of expectancy and electricity. There was a closeness and comradeship among the members because of their common belief in Jesus as the Risen Lord. Their sharing of their faith in love for Jesus resulted in spontaneous sharing of their material possessions. Praise to God and loving concern for each other brought about a rapid growth in church membership. (See Acts 2:44–47.)

Using this as a guideline, we can ask of our own local parish:

1. Are any wonders or signs present here?

2. Do we members know what we believe, and do we share our faith and our lives with each other? When we have problems are we willing to admit, "I hurt. My life isn't

going as it should. I need help"? If someone says these things to me, am I willing to lay aside my own concerns and try to help? Do we really have all things, or even anything, in common?

3. Are our hearts glad and generous? Before saying, "How should I know?" we might consider the ease with which the church budget is met and whether or not we as a parish offer aid to those in need. A quick way to check our "spiritual pulse" is to look at our check stubs and appointment calendar. The way we spend our money and our time reveals our priorities.

4. Is our number growing day by day? Are those who are already members really certain of their salvation, and are they concerned that others accept salvation? If asked, "Have you been saved?" will they answer yes, and if asked, when, do they know that it happened on the first Good Friday around 3:00 in the afternoon?

Praise God, there are churches where the members can answer affirmatively to all or most of these questions. These are churches where Jesus is preached from the pulpit and witnessed about in individual conversations. The members attend study classes on the Christian faith, using the Bible as their textbook, and referring to commentaries and theological books to help their understanding. They share their lives with each other, which means they spend time together in small groups of study and discussion, or one-on-one.

In churches such as these Sunday is the joyous highlight of the week. Members join together to praise and worship the Lord they have experienced during the preceding days. The fellowship is like a family reunion even though the members may have seen each other several times during the week. Visitors to such churches return, attracted by the love and warmth they see and feel.

Unfortunately, to many people the average church is so

different from the early Church, or churches such as are described above, that it is scarcely recognizable. The Rev. Everett (Terry) Fullam, rector of St. Paul's Episcopal Church in Darien, Connecticut, has said that by and large the Church today has been acting in a subnormal manner for so long that subnormal seems normal, and churches like the early Church seem abnormal.

Churches reflect the commitment and faith of the individual members. By our words, deeds, and attitudes, we demonstrate either that we belong to Christ or to ourselves. God has invited us to enter the Kingdom and has provided the gate. Jesus is the gate and His Church is the Kingdom where His blessings are to be experienced.

A rather sobering story is told by Franz Kafka in *The Trial*. A man was instructed to enter a kingdom through a certain gate. He found his way to the gate, but noticed a sentinel guarding the entrance. So he sat down and waited for the sentinel to give him instructions, or to grant permission to enter. The guard did nothing and said nothing. So the man continued to sit, waiting for something to happen. For a whole lifetime he sat. Finally the guard closed the door, and turned to the man. "This door was made for you, and for you alone," he said. "And because you chose not to enter it, it is being closed forever."

How tragic it is when some who find the gate refuse to use it and simply sit outside. We may enter the gate one by one, but we find our destiny in fellowship with others. The Church, like heaven itself, is one of relationships. Bound together by the Holy Spirit and the love of God, we are the Church—God's creation.

FIVE

The Kingdom of Heaven

One of Christianity's best-kept secrets is that it is God's will for us to experience the blessings of the Kingdom of God on earth, as well as in heaven. Jesus taught His disciples, who were the charter members of the Christian Church, to pray, "Thy kingdom come, thy will be done, on earth as it is in heaven." Yet the Church so often fails to teach this. "Repent, for the kingdom of heaven is at hand" (Matthew 4:17) were the words Jesus used to begin His ministry. "He presented himself alive after his passion by many proofs, appearing to them during forty days, and speaking of the kingdom of God" (Acts 1:3) concluded His earthly ministry. If the message of the Kingdom was so important that Jesus began and ended His earthly ministry with it, surely this subject deserves a primary spot in the teaching, preaching, and practice of the Church.

The Psalms give a clearer insight into God's will for our lives than much of the Church's teaching. Psalm 20:4–5 proclaims, "May he grant you your heart's desire, and fulfil all your plans! . . . May the Lord fulfil all your petitions!" Psalm 25:12–13 asks, "Who is the man that fears the Lord?" and then answers, "Him will he instruct in the way that he should choose. He himself shall abide in prosperity, and his children shall possess the land."

C. S. Lewis, in his book, *The Weight of Glory*, writes: "If there lurks in most modern minds the notion that to desire our own good and earnestly hope for the enjoyment of it is a bad thing, I submit that this notion has crept in from Kant and the Stoics, and is no part of the Christian faith. Indeed, if we consider the unblushing promises of reward and the staggering nature of the rewards promised in the Gospels, it would seem that our Lord finds our desires, not too strong, but too weak. We are halfhearted creatures, fooling about with drink and sex and ambition when infinite joy is offered us, like an ignorant child who wants to go on making mudpies in a slum because he cannot imagine what is meant by the offer of a holiday at the sea. We are too easily pleased." When we relegate God's blessings to the "sweet bye and bye," we sell short the love and generosity of God.

Jesus' message of the Kingdom was not something new. The first two chapters of Genesis record that at creation God prepared a kingdom and gave man dominion over it. In this environment God and man would have a good relationship, and all of man's needs would be met. Man's spirit, made in God's image, was to be directed by God and in control of man's body and soul.

The Fall (Genesis 3) describes how temptation entered through man's body and soul and wrested control of his spirit. The forbidden fruit was "good for food . . . a delight to the eyes, and . . . to be desired to make one wise" (Genesis 3:6). The body could not resist the promise of a new taste thrill. The soul, which is the intellect, will, and emotions, was fascinated with the prospect of a titillating peek and a stimulating bit of knowledge. The result of this fiasco was that man was expelled from the kingdom, represented by Eden. This did not change God's original intention. The Bible is a record of God seeking—without coercion—to bring man back into a love relationship with Himself where He could pour out the blessings of the Kingdom on the object of His love.

Although Israel mistakenly concluded that the Kingdom of God was synonymous with their nation and earthly power, they were correct in their unwavering hope that God would establish His Kingdom.

Coming out of such a history, it is not surprising that crowds gathered to hear the message of John the Baptist: "Repent, for the Kingdom of heaven is at hand!" It may have been puzzling to them that his message clearly pointed to a Person acting in the power of the Holy Spirit who would inaugurate the long-awaited Kingdom. "I baptize you with water for repentance, but he who is coming after me is mightier than I, whose sandals I am not worthy to carry; he will baptize you with the Holy Spirit and with fire" (Matthew 3:11).

His call to repentance was a call to turn and go in a different direction, to take a second look at Scripture and the circumstances. We Christians today are as much in need of this message of Jesus and John the Baptist as were the people of their day. Now, as then, a second look reveals things we hadn't noticed before, things that require us to revise our opinions and perhaps change our course of action.

Early in Jesus' ministry, He went into the synagogue in Nazareth, where He had been reared, and stood up to read from the book of Isaiah. " 'The Spirit of the Lord is upon me, because he has anointed me to preach good news to the poor. He has sent me to proclaim release to the captives and recovering of sight to the blind, to set at liberty those who are oppressed, to proclaim the acceptable year of the Lord.' And he closed the book, and [said to the people] ... 'Today this scripture has been fulfilled in your hearing' " (Luke 4:18–21). Jesus was urging His hearers to take a second look at a familiar passage of Scripture.

He wanted them to see Him and His ministry in relation to Isaiah's words about the coming Kingdom. His ministry demonstrated, in word and deed, that God does want the hungry to be fed, the blind to see, and the oppressed to be freed. Jesus had come to restore man to life in the Kingdom, but it was not to be a kingdom of power and might by the world's standards. Rather, it was to be the fulfillment of God's original plan for mankind.

"Seek first his kingdom and his righteousness, and all these things shall be yours as well" (Matthew 6:33) is one of the greatest promises of the Gospel. The things He refers to are food and clothing, which represent all of man's material needs. Jesus' teaching is that God will provide for our physical needs, and the important thing is that we seek His Kingdom. Seeking implies action on our part, instead of passive waiting. It assumes that we believe that God exists, that He loves us, and that a search for His Kingdom will not be fruitless. The emphasis in this teaching is on trusting God, putting Him first in our lives.

This is a realistic piece of advice because it acknowledges that both our spiritual and physical needs must be met if we are to enjoy life in God's Kingdom. Equating poverty with virtue—as some people have done—is a mistake. Tevye says in *Fiddler on the Roof*, "It's no shame to be poor; it's no great honor either." To seek fulfillment in riches is equally futile. In either case, the danger lies in assuming that either condition is necessarily the expression of God's will for us.

The Kingdom that Jesus spoke of in His parables and other teachings was not some vague, other-world fantasy. He was talking to ordinary people about everyday life, and the principles He taught were meant to be applied in the home and in the marketplace. Jesus knew they worked or He wouldn't have taught them.

I can verify from my own experiences that Kingdom

principles are valid and just as relevant today as when Jesus first taught them.

Years ago, long before I learned about Kingdom principles, I made my living in entertainment, working in night clubs, making records, and doing daytime television shows. I decided to start a retirement fund, anticipating retirement at around the age of fifty with plenty of time for leisure and travel. Then when I came into a closer relationship with Jesus Christ, my goals changed dramatically, and I decided to go to college and seminary in order to become an ordained minister. As I began to respond to the pull of God on my life, my own plans and desires were drastically changed, so that it was no problem for me to cash in my retirement fund in order to help with my seminary education. In fact, today the idea of retirement holds absolutely no interest for me, and I hope to continue to do preaching and teaching missions for many more years.

Although the satisfaction and fulfillment that I have received from the ministry would have been enough, Jesus has given me "all these things" that He said would be added—and more. For example, Anne and I have always wanted to travel. Since I have been in the ordained ministry we have visited the British Isles several times, the Holy Land, and many parts of Europe—at no expense to us. We continue to enjoy traveling, and God provides us with ample opportunity for this through the teaching missions that we conduct together. More important than this, God has blessed us through our relationships with our children, grandchildren, friends, and other family members. The things that He has "added unto us" continue to amaze me.

Anne and I have seen the trustworthiness of Jesus' teachings on the Kingdom in church life, as well as in our personal lives. Every church I have served has been different in size, makeup, and needs, yet the truth of Jesus' words about how to enjoy life in the Kingdom has applied to every one of them.

When I was first ordained I served two small "mission" churches. There the emphasis for seeking the Kingdom began with personal spiritual growth. This was undoubtedly something that I needed, and apparently most of the people in those small churches felt that they would like to join me in a struggle toward spiritual maturity. We shared in some excellent study courses. One of the best was called, appropriately, "Journey in Faith." In it, we explored basic questions about man, God, prayer, the sacraments, relationships, and other subjects. We met for Bible study, and we learned to pray together. We got acquainted with one another and shared in a variety of experiences. During this time, we grew numerically to some degree, stewardship increased, and the church facilities were expanded. On looking back, we can see that as we sought the inner Kingdom of God "all these things" that the world labels signs of success were being added to us.

We do not want to imply that those days were all "sweetness and light." Our little congregations were facing things like sons in Vietnam, friends and family in Selma during the civil rights march to Montgomery, and the shock of national assassinations, beginning with the tragic day in November when President Kennedy was killed. This was the same day that we had the first death that I had to deal with in my ministry. I remember hearing the news of Kennedy's death about the same time that a nurse told me my parishioner's little son had died.

It was hard sometimes to hear God's voice in all that was happening, but we were learning that in seeking His Kingdom and His righteousness, we must look for Him *in all things*—not just in matters of "churchy things" of ritual, ceremony, and Sunday school.

Three of our children were teenagers during those years,

and our two younger ones were approaching their teen years. The issues we faced with the older children were the usual ones: dating, grades, friends, drinking, peer pressure, and relationships with parents and with the church. The two most important ingredients for survival were love and trust, and the family structure rested firmly on both of them. The love and trust that we and our children shared were strong because they were based on a mutual love and trust of God. We found that love not only covers a multitude of sins, but also a multitude of mistakes. We parents struggled to understand and help the children, and the children struggled to understand their own feelings and emotions and still maintain a good relationship with us and with each other. It was not particularly easy for any of us, but we all came through intact. Praise God!

Living with five active children in a modest-sized rectory had certain benefits. We learned the importance of living in community; there was no room for prima donnas. The closeness we had as a family spilled out into the church and the town. This experience has been a tremendous help to us in understanding the concept of the church as "community."

Another Kingdom principle that Jesus taught is, "Unless you turn and become like children, you will never enter the kingdom of heaven. Whoever humbles himself like this child, he is the greatest in the kingdom of heaven" (Matthew 18:3–4). Children are eager to learn. They have teachable minds and spirits that are open to instruction, and soak up new information. They usually have humility coupled with curiosity, and an innate trust that allows them to reach out to others. These are the qualities that Jesus tells us we need if we are to enter the Kingdom. He is not talking about some qualities that "earn" our way into heaven. He is speaking of qualities that are needed in order to experience the blessings of the Kingdom here on earth. Without them, we may not even believe there *is* a Kingdom of God.

Anne and I learned more about the principle of childlike faith in the next church we served, in a large city. When we arrived we found several obvious problems. The physical property was in terrible need of repair. The porch and steps leading into the church office and classrooms looked as if they were waiting just long enough for us to arrive before they fell down. The interior furnishings were well worn and rather bleak and drab. The church itself was old and beautiful, but the roof leaked in several places so that on rainy Sundays, worship was accompanied by the steady drip of water hitting strategically placed buckets. The neighborhood reflected the same problems that beset the church. Homes had become rundown, many in need of new roofs and a coat of paint. There were FOR SALE OR RENT signs on many of the buildings in the business area. The church was on a busy thoroughfare, but most of the traffic was going or coming, seldom stopping in this particular area; the thoroughfare's chief legacy to the neighborhood was noise and gas fumes as the cars and trucks hurried past.

The people of this Episcopal parish, however, were steadfast, faithful, loyal church folk. Many had roots in the Anglican Church of England and were descendants of immigrants who had come to America to work in the steel mills. They possessed a tenacity that enabled them to "hang in there" regardless of circumstances. Although the church roll had dwindled over the years, those who remained seemed close to one another and eager to maintain this particular parish.

Many of the church members responded eagerly to Bible classes, as well as to "work parties" to repair the church property. The buildings were spruced up, classes grew, attendance at worship services increased, and there was an air of optimism and renewal among all of us.

A small group of women met weekly for prayer and Bible study, and when Anne joined them she found herself in a ready-made family, a close-knit group of four or five believers. One morning a member of the prayer group arrived late, and was very upset. It seemed one of her neighbors, the mother of several small children, was separated from her husband and supported her family by working in a nearby store. The mother earned a small salary and felt she could not afford to pay for childcare, so she had her school-aged children take turns missing school in order to care for the younger children while she worked. On this particular morning, a small fire had started in the woman's apartment and the neighbors, alerted by the screams of the children, had gone to their rescue. Fortunately no one was hurt, and there was only minor damage to the apartment, but the incident called attention to a problem that this member of the prayer group had not known existed. Here was a family, right in her own block, that was in real need, but no one had known about it. Worse, it was learned from talking to others in the area, the problem was not an isolated one. There were many other single-parent families who could not, or would not, pay for childcare for pre-schoolers and whose older children were without adult supervision for hours each day.

The little prayer group talked about this at length, and prayed for guidance as to what they could do. The answer became clear. The church was in the right location to minister to these families, and there was a large two-story house that belonged to the church that was being used for Sunday school. All agreed: "Let's open a day care center as a service of this parish. We'll run it ourselves and won't charge for our services." All in the group were seeking the Kingdom of God and His righteousness, and were certainly going about it in childlike faith. None of the women knew anything about organizing or operating a day care center, although several had teaching degrees and experience in early childhood education.

Fortunately, as Anne related later, they did not know at first about all the rules and regulations that must be followed in a project like this—things like having so much space per child, so many workers per child, inspection of kitchen facilities, menus that must meet specified standards, and many, many, other requirements. The red tape is extensive, and no one even discussed how such an undertaking was to be financed.

But there is a saying among some Christians that God always pays for what He orders. He must have ordered this day care center, because He certainly brought it into being. Church members responded to the need by offering their services and their money to refurbish the old house to meet the standards set by the state's Day Care Center Board. The members of the prayer group talked to directors of existing day care centers and spent hours visiting other centers and meeting with State Directors. Word spread of what our parish was about, and donations of money and equipment began to come in from other churches and individuals. Flyers were distributed announcing the proposed opening date, and reservations for children began to filter in. There was a strong feeling of wonder and excitement among us all. There had been such a sense that this project was of the Lord, and now we were seeing firsthand the ways He was working to bring it into reality. With every obstacle and frustration we encountered, we seemed to hear Him say, "Trust Me."

The center opened for business, and the children came. The hours were long—from six in the morning until five-thirty or six in the evening, whenever the last child was picked up. The staff consisted of volunteers who worked split shifts. Then, just when it seemed we couldn't manage the demanding schedule and meet our own family obligations, a lovely retired lady who lived nearby applied for full-time work. And all of the volunteers cried, "Amen." Of course, our lady from the Lord couldn't handle the center alone, but her presence meant that the volunteers could have more time at home, plus she gave continuity to the children because she was there every day.

The center operated for several years as a visible witness to the community, and to the church that housed it, of God's love and providence. Finally, as urban renewal came to the area, it gave way to a Head Start Program. We learned from this also. Just because God tells us to do a certain thing in a certain place doesn't mean that He wills for it to continue forever. Change is a part of life, and seeking God's Kingdom in childlike faith means being open to change.

Generally speaking, people are open to change if they think it will improve their situation or pay off in other ways. That is why it is so important for Christians to know the promises of God, see and hear evidence that He makes good on those promises, and then take another look—a second look—at what He says in His manual for living, the Bible.

There are two kinds of faith: salvation faith and Kingdom-living faith, and the two are inseparable. Salvation faith is trusting completely that Jesus died to save us, and knowing that any attempt to save ourselves by doing good works, or being good, is futile, and doomed to failure. We receive salvation when we commit our lives to Jesus Christ as our Savior. Salvation means, first, reconciliation with God and, second, being restored to the love relationship with Him that was broken by our sinful disobedience and the fact that we have shoved Him out of the center of our lives. The Christian life is not a life lived out of duty but one lived out of gratitude for God's mercy and grace. It is a life of privilege and of responsibility.

We have been saved *from* separation from God, which is

what hell is. We have been saved from the fear of dying, the fear of living, and the power of anything to enslave us, of anything to blight the life that God wills for His people. That is the good news. Jesus Christ came, lived, and died, so that we may experience this deliverance. The Christian religion is a relationship with God, established by faith in the Person, power, and program of Jesus Christ. This "saving" religion becomes real to us when we accept Jesus as our personal Savior, and promise to follow Him as our Lord. This is not something that we do just one time. It requires a daily dying to self, looking to Him for deliverance of all kinds, and allowing Him to be in control of our lives.

We have also been saved *for* something. We have been saved for experiencing the blessings of the Kingdom of God on earth, and for spreading it in the world. Saved "from" is salvation faith, saved "for" is Kingdom-living faith. Kingdom living faith manifests the guidance and empowerment of the Holy Spirit, and gives evidence that we are living in the Kingdom. The blessings of the Kingdom are:

First, *peace*—a peace that comes from God. It does not mean, necessarily, the absence of strife of any kind. It is a sense of well-being in spite of outward circumstances. This is what the Middle Eastern word *shalom* means. This peace comes from the conviction that God is in control, and that He is able to keep His promises—and will keep them.

Second, *joy*—a joy that is founded on the trustworthiness and love of God, as expressed in Jesus Christ. It comes from knowing Him as personal Savior, that we are in the right relationship with God, and that He wills nothing but the best for us.

Third, *power*—power that is not our own, a supernatural power that is a gift from God the Holy Spirit. This is the power to be what we have been reborn to be, and to do what Christ has commissioned us to do.

The world seeks peace and longs for joy, but tries to find

them in everything except the one thing that is necessary—commitment to Jesus as Lord and Savior. Natural man seeks power in the things of the world, but real power comes from God. Jesus' words about seeking the Kingdom are, in my opinion, second only to the promise of salvation in importance. When Christians trust God, commit themselves to Jesus, and open themselves to the guidance and empowerment of the Holy Spirit, they find what has been promised.

Yet, this is only the first part of Kingdom living. The second is to acknowledge and accept our status as members of a ministering body, called to manifest and spread the Kingdom of God in the world.

SIX

The Keys
of the Kingdom

It is within the Church that the Kingdom is meant to be experienced, and the key to the Kingdom is Jesus Christ. In Him, God provided the way for man to come home—to reenter the realm that was forfeited through Adam and Eve's transgression. The Kingdom, like salvation, is a gift, and to enjoy either requires action on man's part. A gift is of no benefit unless it is received and put to use.

When Jesus asked His disciples who they thought He was, He was asking for a response to Himself and to what they had observed as His ministry. Simon Peter's answer was, "You are the Christ, the Son of the living God" (Matthew 16:16). The other disciples had been with Jesus just as Peter had, but it was Peter who received the divine revelation. "Blessed are you, Simon Bar-Jona! For flesh and blood has not revealed this to you, but my Father who is in heaven" (Matthew 16:17).

Leon Morris, principal of Ridley College in Melbourne, Australia, states in his book, *I Believe in Revelation*, that the recipient of such revelation sees the same things that others do, but with an extra dimension. "He sees not only what the other man sees, but he also perceives what God is disclosing to him in the situation."

Peter's perception of who Jesus was, and his courage in speaking it forth, led Jesus to declare, "You are Peter, and on this rock I will build my church, and the powers of death shall not prevail against it. I will give you the keys of the kingdom of heaven, and whatever you bind on earth shall be bound in heaven, and whatever you loose on earth shall be loosed in heaven" (Matthew 16:18–19). The terms "bind" and "loose" were technical terms of the rabbis meaning forbid and permit, and the symbol of the keys was used to show authority in the household of God. Jesus told Peter that this authority would be on earth as well as in heaven. He spoke of a Kingdom that would begin on earth and continue in heaven.

The first Beatitude is another reference to this Kingdom. "Blessed are the poor in spirit, for theirs is the kingdom of heaven" (Matthew 5:3). To be poor in spirit is the opposite of feeling self-sufficient. Jesus says that the poor in spirit are blessed because they are open to hearing and believing the principles of the Kingdom. Although the most familiar definitions of "blessed" are holy, sacred, fortunate, and joyful, it can also mean chosen. The angel, in addressing Mary to tell her she would bear the Christ Child, said, "Blessed are you among women" (Luke 1:42, KJV), for Mary had been chosen by God. Using "blessed" as "chosen" emphasizes God's desire for us to enjoy Kingdom living. He has chosen anyone who will accept His Son for this privilege. Choosing to accept Jesus as Savior is the first step in seeking the Kingdom. Enjoying the Kingdom means using the keys of the Kingdom to open the Kingdom's treasures.

In St. Luke's Gospel, after Jesus tells the disciples to seek the Kingdom, He adds, "Fear not, little flock, for it is your Father's good pleasure to give you the kingdom" (12:32).

Anyone who has ever offered a gift to someone can understand that the real pleasure in giving comes when the gift is received and enjoyed. It is the Father's pleasure to give, and our blessing to receive.

When the Pharisees asked when this Kingdom was coming, Jesus answered, "The kingdom of God is not coming with signs to be observed; nor will they say, 'Lo, here it is!' or 'There!' for behold, the kingdom of God is in the midst of you" (Luke 17:20–21). The King James Version reads, "The kingdom of God . . . is within you." Both of these translations may be taken in a literal sense, because the Kingdom of God is experienced both in the gathered community of believers and in the individual heart.

The best way to understand what Jesus is talking about when He refers to the Kingdom is to study His parables. Over one-third of His recorded words are parables, and many of these are on the Kingdom. The Kingdom parables bring us into direct contact with the mind of Christ, for all of them show the grace of God, and describe the Christian life.

When Jesus—the Word of God—speaks to us it is to tell us who He is, and what His purposes are. In His mercy He speaks often through images and figures that are familiar to us. The parables, in their concrete examples of grain, fruit, pearls, lamps, and such, give us the comforting certainty that God is not some remote, inaccessible "other" who is beyond us, but One who is concerned with everything around us. Jesus uses the physical realities of commonplace objects to illustrate spiritual truths and to help us grow in our relationships with God through giving us glimpses of the Kingdom of heaven.

Two of Jesus' parables indicate that people enter the Kingdom in different ways. In the first, the parable of the treasure hidden in a field, Jesus says that the man found and covered up the treasure. Then, in his joy, he goes and sells all that he has and buys the field (Matthew 13:44). This sounds as if the man stumbled upon the treasure, but did not immediately take it. Later, to his joy, he realized its worth, and sold all that he had in order to possess it. Perhaps this is the story of lifelong church members who may hear the Gospel Sunday after Sunday before they finally realize its worth and reorder their priorities in order to receive it into their lives. Once a person gets a taste of the Kingdom, it whets his appetite for more.

I believe that it is possible to experience the blessings of the Kingdom without even realizing that there is something that is called a Kingdom. This is particularly true of people who are living on "spiritual welfare." They enjoy the results of the commitment of others. They are the beneficiaries of what the corporate body of believers is accomplishing. It has been said that many men have their religion in their wives' names, just as they often, for business reasons, put their property in their wives' names. Nevertheless, sometimes these "spiritual welfare" recipients become committed Christians because of the glimpses they get of the Kingdom in the lives of others.

In my own case, I experienced the blessings of the Kingdom for years before I realized that there is a Kingdom with its blessings available here on earth. I had been a nominal Christian from the time I was twelve years old. Although I had a happy childhood, it was not until I married that the— at the time—unidentified blessings of the Kingdom began to manifest themselves. I had a good, beautiful wife, five fine children, a profession that offered good money and a modicum of gratifying fame. We were involved in a parish where Jesus was preached and the Bible was taught. As we reaped some of the spiritual blessings of the Kingdom, along with the material ones, we were filled with gratitude and a bit awed by the goodness of God. After several years, God gave me a little "divine discontent" with show business, which led me to take a second look at how I wanted to spend the rest of my life. Experiencing the Kingdom's blessings, combined with a deepening commitment to the Lord, will usually lead a person to search for ways to serve Him. Although there are many ways to serve God, I felt led to follow the route to the ordained ministry. During the years of college and seminary education we continued to receive financial rewards, a good relationship with our children, and new lasting friendship with various committed Christians.

Our twenty years in the parish ministry have been enjoyable and productive. During eighteen of those years I conducted well over two hundred and fifty teaching missions in thirty-three states. My wife and I wrote three books based on these teachings and today are conducting teaching missions together on a full-time basis. Like the man in the parable, I stumbled into the Kingdom without even looking for it. I praise God that this is possible and I thank Him that it happened to me.

The second parable, of the merchant who found the pearl of great value, is about a man who *was* searching for something worthwhile in life. It does not record what "fine pearls" he tried before he discovered the one pearl that was worth selling all that he had in order to possess it. Whatever he sought, this man finally realized that there was only one thing that could give him the fulfillment that would make life more than mere existence. This parable reminds us of Jesus' words to his friend Martha. "Martha, Martha, you are anxious and troubled about many things; one thing is needful. Mary has chosen the good portion, which shall not be taken away from her" (Luke 10:41–42). Mary had the discernment to know that if she made her Lord the center of her life, all of the other things would fall into place. This was truly a case of "first things first."

Two other parables teach that the presence of the Kingdom will be visible to others. In the parable of the mustard seed, the smallest of all seeds grows into the greatest of shrubs, and birds of the air come and make nests in its branches (Matthew 13:31–32). When the Kingdom is present, the blessings can be enjoyed by others. The same point is made in the parable of the leaven that a woman hid in three measures of meal. The leaven was not distinguishable from the meal, but it did a work that affected the entire loaves (Matthew 13:33). In the earliest beginnings of the Church the Kingdom was visible. The pagans used to say, "See how those Christians love one another." In the Dark Ages, monasteries gave evidence of its presence. I feel that it was the prayers and the services rendered by the religious in those dark days that may have been instrumental in holding the world together. Hospitals and leper colonies also have often shown the pagan world that the Kingdom can be present even under the most difficult conditions.

In the parable of the wheat and the tares (Matthew 13:24–30), Jesus warns that in this life there will always be weeds alongside the grain, but we are not to judge, "lest in gathering the weeds you root up the wheat along with them." A judgmental spirit has no place in the Kingdom of God. There were people who, in my younger days, certainly could have considered me a tare. Fortunately, many people who are not "Bible-toting" Christians have the seed of the Gospel growing slowly inside them. We should never underestimate the power of Christian leaven in a person's life.

We cannot overemphasize the importance of forgiveness if we are to enjoy life in the Kingdom. Jesus stressed this in His parable on forgiveness (Matthew 18:23–35). He tells of a king who wished to settle accounts with his servants. When a man who owed him ten thousand talents could not pay, the king ordered him and his family to be sold and payment made. The man begged for mercy, promising to pay later, and the king, out of pity, "forgave him the debt." The debt was so great that the king knew the man would never be able to pay it. Later, when a fellow servant could not pay the forgiven man a much, much smaller debt, he had him thrown into prison. The king heard of this, and sent for the man he had forgiven. "You wicked servant! I forgave you all that debt because you besought me; and should not you have had mercy on your fellow servant, as I had mercy on you?" The King James Version ends this story with the words, "And his lord was wroth, and delivered him to the tormentors, till he should pay all that was due unto him" (Matthew 18:34). The king may be compared to God who has forgiven us a debt that we could never be able to pay and we are, in turn, to forgive those who have wronged us. Figuratively speaking, but theologically correct, on the Cross of Jesus, God wrote, "Debt canceled."

This parable makes it clear that the debts of sin are valid and forgiveness is an act of grace. Forgiveness is a matter of the will, not the emotions. It is not a question of forgiving and forgetting; it is simply the act of canceling the debt. It is true today, just as in the parable, that when we refuse to forgive someone, it eats away at us; we are truly "delivered to the tormentors" whether it takes the form of headaches, high blood pressure, upset stomachs, or ulcers. Many churches have split over some petty argument or hurt feelings caused by the refusal to forgive. Many people are under siege by "tormentors" because they just "can't forgive." When we say, "I can't forgive," we really mean, "I won't forgive." History reveals that wars are fought because refusal to forgive moves from individuals to groups, and on to nations.

Throughout His dealings with man, God has made it clear that love is the primary attribute of the Kingdom. Jesus summarizes this in the words, "You shall love the Lord your God with all your heart, and with all your soul, and with all your mind . . . [and] you shall love your neighbor as yourself. On these two commandments depend all the law and the prophets" (Matthew 22:37–40). The Kingdom on earth, like the Kingdom in heaven, is one of right relationships between man and God, and man and man. This results in the absence of fear and anxiety, and the presence of joy, peace, and power.

St. Paul speaks of this often. "For the kingdom of God is not food and drink but righteousness and peace and joy in the Holy Spirit" (Romans 14:17). "For the kingdom of God does not consist in talk but in power" (1 Corinthians 4:20). "For God did not give us a spirit of timidity but a spirit of power and love and self-control" (2 Timothy 1:7). Such an atmosphere is conducive for all kinds of healing.

God wants His people healthy and whole. Jesus acknowledged the presence of disease and illness in this fallen world, but never refused to heal. He sent the Twelve out "to preach the kingdom of God and to heal" (Luke 9:2). Later He appointed seventy others and sent them to "heal the sick . . . and say to them, 'The kingdom of God has come near to you' " (Luke 10:9). The book of Acts records that the early Church continued Jesus' ministry of preaching, teaching, and healing.

The Church, which is the Kingdom of God on earth, is meant to be a healing fellowship that works in conjunction with the medical profession. Just as the medical profession uses resources that God provides, the Church must use its resources of prayer, faith, the laying on of hands, and the anointing with oil. The letter of James states this plainly: "Is any among you sick? Let him call for the elders of the church, and let them pray over him, anointing him with oil in the name of the Lord; and the prayer of faith will save the sick man, and the Lord will raise him up; and if he has committed sins, he will be forgiven" (James 5:14–15).

This gift of the Kingdom and all its attendant blessings can be our own. Jesus, the glorious key, has swung the door open before us and will lead us through. We have but to choose to follow Him, for as we will see in the next chapter, it is possible to miss the Kingdom.

SEVEN

The Principles
of the Kingdom

The parable of the sower, or as it is sometimes called, the parable of the soils, is a story on the exercise of understanding. It is recorded in the first three Gospels, and of it Jesus asked the disciples, "Do you not understand this parable? How then will you understand all the parables?" (Mark 4:13). He was implying that this parable unlocks the mystery of the Kingdom and presents us with the principles that are the means of entering into the Kingdom and experiencing its blessings.

Jesus told this parable at a high point in His life and ministry. The crowds were so great that He had to get into a boat to speak. The beach was filled with people who had been listening to Jesus teach about the Kingdom of God. He had been sowing the Word, and then He told a parable of how frequently this divine seed is destroyed or rejected, in spite of the great rewards it promises. This parable is found in Luke 8:5–15.

"A sower went out to sow his seed." The seed is the Word of God, and the parable opens with a very practical statement. If the sower expects a crop, the first step must be to plant the seed. This is a lesson the Church can learn from every farmer or gardener.

"And as he sowed, some fell along the path, and was trodden under foot, and the birds of the air devoured it." The path that received the seed was not prepared for it. The pounding of many feet had formed a hard, smooth surface. A busy thoroughfare is not the sort of place that is a likely spot to plant a garden. When we are too preoccupied with activities, no matter how useful they are, we become like this path. We are too hard and packed down to receive God's Word, no matter how often it is thrown at us.

In such a situation, it is inevitable that "birds" of one kind or another will take the seed. Genesis tells us that when birds of prey came down to eat the carcasses of the sacrificial animals that were to seal a covenant between God and Abram, Abram was forced to drive them away (Genesis 15:11). Both of these stories show that it is our responsibility to drive away anything that would steal our heritage from us. God doesn't want us to be helpless victims of life, but rather to exercise the dominion He has given us, and to be active participants in the Kingdom that Jesus offers.

"The ones along the path are those who have heard; then the devil comes and takes away the word from their hearts, that they may not believe and be saved." In this explanation of the first kind of soil, Jesus states that unless we receive the Word inside us, we are in danger of missing salvation. How can we believe and be saved unless we hear and understand the Word of God? It is always the aim of Satan to chip away at our faith in order to lead us away from God. Jesus had experienced temptation to doubt God while he was in the wilderness, so he knew firsthand of this danger. His defense had been to combat the words of the devil by using the words of Scripture.

When the Word of God fails to sink in and bring light and direction, it may not always be due to lack of interest or understanding. There are other forces at work in the world whose purpose is to snatch away the divine seed and keep it from taking root. This parable gives a clear warning that we must realize this, and deliberately fight them off, just as Abram drove away the birds of prey that tried to eat his offering. The person who naively believes that this is not true is a sitting duck for the devil.

"And some fell on the rock; and as it grew up, it withered away, because it had no moisture." A thin layer of camouflage covered this rock, so it looked promising: a good place to sow seed. Beneath this topsoil there could be rocks of resentment, unforgiveness, fault-finding, apathy, or some recurring sin that the hearer refuses to abandon. This underlying rock causes the soil to be shallow and unable to hold moisture, so whatever grows there will wither.

"And the ones on the rock are those who, when they hear the word, receive it with joy; but these have no root, they believe for a while and in time of temptation fall away." Regardless of how glorious a conversion experience we may have, or how glowing an encounter with the Lord, our enthusiasm will wilt unless we dig out the rocks we may be harboring and take root in the teaching and fellowship of a Christian body of believers. Growth is a lifetime process and no one can manage it alone. We need other people in our Christian journey. We also need a place where we can give as well as receive if the Word of God is to take root in us and produce good fruit.

Helmut Thielicke describes this second type of soil in *The Waiting Father* as those who let Jesus only halfway into their hearts, and he believes that they are far poorer than the one hundred percent worldling. He explains that they do not get the peace that passes understanding, and they also lose the world's peace. Because they have had a taste of spiritual truth, there remains a constant nagging in the heart. A confrontation with Jesus demands that a choice be made, and even if we choose against following Him, we are never quite the way we were. Dr. Sam Shoemaker has described these people as those who have been inoculated with just enough Christianity to prevent them from really catching it.

"And some fell among thorns; and the thorns grew with it and choked it." These are people who receive the seed, and the seed grows well. Their problem is neither indifference to the Word nor shallowness. "But as they go on their way they are choked by the cares and riches and pleasures of life, and their fruit does not mature." Every church has experience with this type of soil. The people it represents may be fine, dedicated church members. They often assume leadership roles and add greatly to the life of the church—for a while. Then they begin to drift away, attending worship services and other functions less frequently, and finally disappearing from the scene.

What happens to them? Many times their friends at church are puzzled and worried by their absence. When they call to ask what is wrong, they are given vague, evasive answers. Sometimes these dropouts will attend another church for a while, but often they simply stop going to any church.

In Jesus' explanation of this type of soil, He says that it is the cares and riches and pleasures of the world that keep the fruit from maturing. This summer I saw an example of this as I watched a neighbor's cornfield grow. The stalks were strong and green, and the ears of corn began to form. Before they could mature, however, the field was invaded by squirrels. The pesky little creatures enjoyed the corn cafeteria-style, skipping from one ear to nibble on the next, and never eating an entire ear. Finally, in disappointment and disgust, the neighbor plowed the crop under. Because the fruit did not mature, the crop was useless.

Squirrels are not evil. They are just out of place in a corn-field. The fault was not that squirrels like to eat, but that the farmer could not find a way to control them. Something was out of order. God did not give squirrels dominion over man, but instead instructed man to have dominion over every living creature.

The cares and riches and pleasures of life are not evil, either. Trouble comes when they are not kept in their proper order—when we allow them to control us as the squirrels controlled the cornfield.

Some cares of the world—earning a living, rearing a family, meeting unexpected obstacles in relationships, or any other part of life that could be considered a "care"—often help us move toward maturity, instead of hindering us. I believe that the cares that Jesus warns against are more often some sort of bondage to the past.

This can take several forms. A poor self-image usually has roots in some painful childhood experiences. The person who doesn't like and respect himself has difficulty liking and respecting others. The result can be seen in hurt feelings, resentment toward others, and resistance to authority. A critical nature is a sign of a poor self-image.

Another bondage to the past can be seen in fear of change. It is so easy to fantasize the "good old days." The song "Camelot" appeals to people because it tells of a place where the climate is perfect, everybody gets along with everybody else, and trouble never rears its ugly head. The fact that this "fleeting wisp of glory" never existed does not deter those who are chained to the past. It does make it very traumatic for them when the inevitable changes take place. This pain seems to be most acute when change occurs in the church. "But that's not the way we've always done it!" becomes a battle hymn or a funeral dirge, depending upon the personality of the sufferer.

The thorns of bondage to the past are present in everyone's life. None of us is immune. They do us harm only when we allow them to take over, and prevent us from becoming mature Christians. This is another area in which we need the Christian community to help us keep the past and the present in the right balance. The past is not necessarily bad. In fact, to quote a cliché, "The person who ignores the past is doomed to keep repeating its mistakes." We can learn from the past, but we must also be willing to move into the present and toward the future. This is maturity.

The riches and pleasures of life, Jesus warned, can also prevent us from producing mature fruit. Again, it is a matter of priority. As long as they are not the axis around which our life revolves, they are not dangerous. The Bible makes it clear that God loves us, and wants us to enjoy life in His Kingdom. The redemption that Jesus offers can extend to the material realm just as to the spiritual and emotional realms. Unless this happens, though, the price that these thorns will exact is immaturity. Maturity means to be fully developed, perfected. The person who fails to mature does not live up to his potential. He settles for less than God intends him to be. One definition of sin is missing the mark. This is the sin of immaturity. In such cases, it is inevitable that when temptation comes the person falls away. More people disappear from churches because of petty differences of opinion or resistance to change than for theological reasons.

"And some fell into good soil and grew, and yielded a hundredfold." Jesus explains that these are people who "hearing the word, hold it fast in an honest and good heart, and bring forth fruit with patience."

At different times we are each of the four types of soil, but it is this last type that brings fulfillment and peace to us, and gives glory to God. This is the soil that *will* produce fruit. A return is promised. Some of the Gospels say it can be thirtyfold, or sixtyfold, or even a hundredfold. The amount may differ, but there will definitely be a return.

To hold the Word fast in an honest and good heart means

to think about it, meditate on it, and believe that it is a word
for our own lives. Mary, the mother of Jesus, gives a good
example of how this works. After Jesus was born, the shepherds came to worship Him. They told Mary and Joseph of
how the angels had appeared to them, praising God and
saying, "Glory to God in the highest, and on earth peace
among men with whom he is pleased!" (Luke 2:14).

This must have seemed puzzling to Mary. There was little
evidence of peace or good will in the world she knew. She
had just given birth in alien and unfamiliar surroundings,
far from home. The words of these rough shepherds
couldn't have made much sense to her, yet "Mary kept all
these things, pondering them in her heart" (Luke 2:19).
Then she complied with all the Jewish customs. The child
was circumcised on the eighth day, He was called by the
name the angel had given Mary before He was conceived,
and sacrifices were offered at His presentation in the Temple. When Joseph told her that he had been warned in a
dream to flee into Egypt with her and the child, she went
without questioning. Because of her honest and good heart,
Mary was able to hear the Word of God in the words of the
shepherds, of Simeon and Anna in the Temple who recognized Jesus as the Christ, and of Joseph. Mary held fast to
the Word, even when she did not understand.

This parable of the sower promises that all who hear the
Word of God, and hold it fast in an honest and good heart,
will, like Mary, bring forth fruit, with patience. Mary had to
go through periods of doubt, uncertainty, and finally see her
beloved son put to death, before the resurrection brought
forth the fruit that was the salvation of the world. Through
it all, she held fast.

To hold fast to the Word means to trust God in spite of
the circumstances. It may mean to recognize those in need
as my neighbors, and to see in my cantankerous church
brethren children of God, brothers or sisters in Christ. To

hold fast to the Word means that I put my trust in its ability to do what it promises, so that the Word itself accepts the responsibility for the things I do in His name.

This parable makes it clear that the blessings of the Kingdom cannot be had cheaply. They require repentance on our part, and a desire to allow God to change and mold us into the kind of people who glorify Him and bless other people. When these are present, the principles become fairly simple to follow.

The first is the principle of sowing in order to reap. This is taught throughout the New Testament. The Golden Rule is one version: If you want people to be nice to you, you must be nice to them. If you want more friends, "plant" friendship through acts of consideration and kindness to others. Whatever you desire or need, this principle teaches that in order to receive we must first give. Jesus' words underlie this principle: "Give, and it will be given to you; good measure, pressed down, shaken together, running over, will be put into your lap. For the measure you give will be the measure you get back" (Luke 6:38). This applies to money as well as to love and friendship. The only place in the Bible where we are urged to test God is in the area of giving away money—tithing. Malachi 3:10–12 urges, "Bring the full tithes into the storehouse, that there may be food in my house; and *thereby put me to the test*, says the Lord of hosts, if I will not open the windows of heaven for you and pour down for you an overflowing blessing. I will rebuke the devourer for you, so that it will not destroy the fruits of your soil; and your vine in the field shall not fail to bear, says the Lord of hosts. Then all nations will call you blessed, for you will be a land of delight, says the Lord of hosts." This is a promise that does not change.

There is a church in Bristol, England, that is living proof of this. St. Philip and St. Jacob's, affectionately called "Pip and Jay," is a beautiful old structure, but over the years the

74

membership had declined drastically. In 1963 the average evening attendance was about thirty-five. In 1964 a small group of young people began to support the church, and a young vicar was assigned to serve them. In June 1965, the Bishop of Bristol told them that unless membership and attendance doubled, and giving increased proportionately within three years, the church would be closed for worship and remain only as a historic relic for sightseers.

The vicar and his little congregation decided to claim God's promise that if they put His Kingdom first, He would meet their material needs. Bible study and prayer meetings, plus an openness to the empowerment of the Holy Spirit, were the groundwork for this. The first year they gave away £187 and kept 500 for repairs to the church and "at home" needs. Two years later they gave away £768 keeping 772. In 1971 the amount given away was £4422 while keeping 2080. These figures do not include additional giving to the diocese.

Membership has increased along with the spiritual and financial growth. In 1982, when Anne and I visited this church, they were supporting twelve missionaries, in addition to their inner city outreach, and giving to a number of missionary societies worldwide. They continue to have weekly prayer meetings and Bible studies, and have added half-nights of intercessory prayer as needed. There is an aliveness and warmth in the worship services, and the members exhibit love and hospitality. We stayed in the home of parishioners during our visit who took us into their family life as if we were lifelong friends. The same minister who was there in 1964 is the priest, and he told us that over the years God has never failed to meet their needs—in fact, he said, they find it impossible to outgive God. The more they give away, the more they receive.

2. Another principle found in this parable is the power of words. The parable teaches that the seed is the Word of

God, and the power to reproduce lies in the seed. The same is true of our own words. They are powerful, and will produce good or bad, according to whether positive or negative words are spoken. Solomon wrote: "From the fruit of his mouth a man is satisfied; he is satisfied by the yield of his lips. Death and life are in the power of the tongue, and those who love it will eat its fruits" (Proverbs 18:20–21). The child who is constantly told he is clumsy or stupid grows into an inept and unproductive adult. The person who continually moans about how bad business is often ends in bankruptcy. The suspicious wife who keeps accusing her husband of being unfaithful should not be surprised when he finally leaves her for another woman.

Since this is a principle that works as surely as the law of gravity does, we are wise to use it in a positive way. It can become as easy to speak affirming words as condemning ones. This is not being dishonest. It is speaking things into being. It is following the example of God who "calls into existence the things that do not exist" (Romans 4:17). God called Abraham the father of many nations while he was still childless. Jesus called Peter the rock on which the Church would be built, even though he knew Peter would deny him out of cowardice and run away. There are many times when we can speak positive words about something that has not yet happened. The person who says, "I am getting well" is far more likely to return to health than the one who declares, "I'll probably never be well again."

Peter was using this principle of the power of words when he made his first confession of faith in Jesus as the Christ, the Son of the living God. Just believing was not enough. He had to speak his belief. Romans 10:10 makes a strong statement about this: "For man believes with his heart and so is justified, and he confesses with his lips and so is saved."

Most Christians do not question that there is power in God's Word, but many do not realize the power that is in our words as well. They can create or destroy, and they reveal more about the state of our spiritual and emotional health than we care to admit. "Out of the abundance of the heart the mouth speaks" (Matthew 12:34) is another way of saying that our words reflect our feelings. The beautiful thing about recognizing this principle is that we can choose to speak our way into changing our attitudes, instead of just waiting until we feel good to say something positive.

There is order and continuity in God's created world. We see examples of cause and effect in the natural world, and we learn to adjust our lives to them. The same is true in the Kingdom of heaven on earth. As we learn to recognize the principles of this Kingdom, and practice them in practical ways, we are simply opening ourselves to receive the blessings that God wants to give us.

The first step in doing this is to make it a practice to read and meditate on Scripture and, when possible, to attend Bible study classes. This is the way we plant the Word in our hearts. Jesus promised that the Word will bear fruit when we do this. As we plant verses such as "And my God will supply every need of yours according to his riches in glory in Christ Jesus" (Philippians 4:19) and "The Lord is the strength of his people . . ." (Psalm 28:8), we are planting the seeds of peace, trust, and faith in God. This principle of planting God's Word reaps strength for the individual Christian and the corporate body of the Church.

To summarize, the secret of the Kingdom is in "sowing and reaping," and the principles are:

1. Our spirit is the soil.
2. The seed is the Word—both God's and ours.
3. The power is in the seed.
4. We must sow in order to reap. (This is true of everything.)

5. We reap whatever it is that we sow, good or bad.

6. A return is guaranteed.

Some of these principles work in the secular world, and for nonreligious people, because a principle is a fundamental truth or law on which others are based. The point Jesus was making in this parable is that to enjoy the blessings of the Kingdom, Christians must apply these principles to every aspect of life.

EIGHT

God's
Three-Legged Stool

The idea of referring to the Church as God's footstool comes from the Bible. First Chronicles 28:2 says, "Then King David rose to his feet and said: 'Hear me, my brethren and my people. I had it in my heart to build a house of rest for the ark of the covenant of the Lord, and for the footstool of our God; and I made preparations for building.' " There are several such references in the Psalms, such as Psalm 132:7: "Let us go to his dwelling place; let us worship at his footstool!"

In this book we use this analogy to describe the Church, and point out that a footstool must have legs to support it. Although the Church is built on the foundation of Jesus Christ, God in His wisdom has provided three legs, or disciplines, to aid the Church in fulfilling its two basic functions: worship and service. The Church must stand firmly on the three legs—the Sacramental, the Evangelical, and the Pentecostal—if it is to do what it was created to do. References to these three disciplines can be found throughout both the Old and New Testaments.

In the Old Testament, the building of altars to commemorate spiritual encounters with God, deliverances from some physical danger, and for the sacrifice of animals were examples of the Sacramental leg. The Pentecostal leg was seen whenever God's Spirit communicated with the people through individual encounters such as Abraham and Moses enjoyed, or through the messages the prophets received from Him. Events such as the burning bush, the parting of the Red Sea, and the feeding with manna and quail were supernatural demonstrations of the Pentecostal leg that God provided for His covenant people. The Evangelical leg was seen in the frequent retelling—by witnessing and teaching—of the mighty acts of God: "And these words which I command you this day shall be upon your heart; and you shall teach them diligently to your children, and shall talk of them when you sit in your house, and when you walk by the way, and when you lie down, and when you rise" (Deuteronomy 6:6–7).

This threefold emphasis continues in the New Testament. The magnificent words in the opening chapter of John's Gospel set the scene for the sacramental nature of Jesus' life and ministry. "And the Word became flesh and dwelt among us, full of grace and truth; we have beheld his glory, glory as of the only Son from the Father" (John 1:14). This theme began with His entrance into human history, continued with His institution of the sacraments of Christian baptism and Holy Communion, and climaxed with Jesus' sacrificial death on the Cross.

All four Gospels highlight the Pentecostal leg of Jesus' ministry. From the beginning to the end of His earthly ministry Jesus operated through the power of the Holy Spirit. Changing water into wine, the healings, the miraculous feedings, and the Transfiguration are some evidences of this.

Jesus stressed the importance of the Evangelical leg from the time He called Peter and Andrew to be His disciples. "Follow me, and I will make you fishers of men" (Matthew

4:19). Later, His command to "go into all the world and preach the gospel to the whole creation" (Mark 16:15) expanded the call to evangelism.

Finally, in Matthew 28:19–20, Jesus incorporates the Sacramental, the Pentecostal, and the Evangelical disciplines in the Great Commission: "Go therefore and make disciples of all nations, baptizing them in the name of the Father and of the Son and of the Holy Spirit, teaching them to observe all that I have commanded you; and lo, I am with you always, to the close of the age."

That great book on the Church, Paul's letter to the Ephesians, continues the Biblewide recognition of the three legs that are intended to nourish, empower, and guide the Church in its worship and its Great Commission. Paul recognizes the Evangelical leg in the first verse of the first chapter when he refers to himself as "an apostle of Christ Jesus by the will of God" and to the Ephesian Church as "saints who are also faithful in Christ Jesus." The word *apostle* means "one who is sent," and Paul's evangelistic zeal encouraged the early Church to be faithful to this call to spread the good news of Jesus Christ. His insight into God's plan for uniting all things in God (Ephesians 1:10) gave him a unique appreciation of the Evangelical leg, and he urged the early Church to remember, "We are his workmanship, created in Christ Jesus for good works, which God prepared beforehand, that we should walk in them" (Ephesians 2:10). Paul continues this evangelistic theme when he speaks of his call "to preach to the Gentiles the unsearchable riches of Christ" (Ephesians 3:8).

Paul refers to the Pentecostal leg when he writes: "In him you also, who have heard the word of truth, the gospel of your salvation, and have believed in him, were sealed with the promised Holy Spirit, which is the guarantee of our inheritance until we acquire possession of it, to the praise of his glory" (Ephesians 1:13–14). A few verses later Paul writes that he prays for the Ephesian church to manifest some of the gifts of the Holy Spirit—wisdom, revelation, and knowledge (Ephesians 1:17)—in order to fully understand its call. The entire fourth chapter emphasizes the Pentecostal leg, as Paul speaks extensively of the gifts of the Holy Spirit that are given for the building up of the Body of Christ, and concludes with a plea: "Do not grieve the Holy Spirit of God, in whom you were sealed for the day of redemption" (Ephesians 4:30).

The Christian sacrament of baptism finds much of its theology in the second chapter of Ephesians in Paul's theme of death because of sin and new life in Christ. Baptism represents drowning and rebirth as the new convert sacramentalizes his acceptance of Jesus as Lord and Savior. In the fourth chapter, Paul reminds the Church that there is "one Lord, one faith, one baptism . . ." (Ephesians 4:5). Paul's constant emphasis upon salvation by grace shows that he had a clear concept of the sacramental nature of the Cross and the importance of the Sacramental leg of the Church.

All three legs are needed if the Church is to be the ministering body that represents Christ in its mission and ministry to the world. It seems, however, that each of three major Church branches seems to be trying to balance on only one or two legs rather than all three in its denomination or fellowship.

Historically, the first of these, the Catholic Churches—Roman, Eastern Orthodox, and Anglican—have relied almost entirely on the Sacramental leg and not placed much importance on the Evangelical and Pentecostal legs—the Bible, preaching Jesus, promoting evangelism, and reliance on the Holy Spirit. I once had an elderly Episcopalian tell me that she had never understood about the Holy Spirit, so she just "ignored it." Calling Him an "it" gave ample proof that what she said was certainly true. While the sacraments are vital for proper participation in the worship, work, and life of the church, they cannot compensate for the equally important and necessary contributions of the Evangelical and Pentecostal legs of the church.

Then, there are some denominations that are almost exclusively Evangelical. They are firmly Bible-oriented, although sometimes this orientation tends to skip over certain parts of the Bible. They have strong programs of evangelism and outreach, and excellent programs within the church to nurture the members. Many of these churches grow spectacularly, but the members must depend on their own strength without the strengthening, nourishing power of the sacraments or calling upon the Holy Spirit's power and gifts in work and worship.

Then again, because of the dearth of teaching on the Holy Spirit elsewhere, there are still other denominations whose emphasis is almost entirely on the Pentecostal leg. The Bible is used, but because only certain parts are emphasized, imbalance results. The members may go unnourished by the sacraments, and outreach is limited due to the overemphasis on the necessity of a Pentecostal experience that must be accompanied by evidences—particularly speaking in tongues.

Any denomination, parish, or individual that neglects one or more of the three legs on which the Church stands is *incomplete*. The leg or two on which it stands may be valid, but the lack of the leg or legs that it ignores diminishes its strength. Because of this, much of the power of the Christian faith is untapped.

In recent years there has been a strong growth of nondenominational churches in America and other countries. Their existence is primarily due to members of mainline denominations who recognize that something is lacking in their lives and in their parishes. They feel that there must be something more than what they have been experiencing. Often the most recognized need is for good Bible teaching and there is a powerful and vigorous emphasis on the Evangelical leg in these churches. Out of that Bible teaching comes the realization of the importance of the sacraments, and because sound Bible study discloses the work of the Holy Spirit throughout the history of God's dealings with man, there is usually an emphasis upon the baptism in the Holy Spirit as well. The fact that these churches are growing so fast points up the failure of many mainline churches to utilize all three legs of God's ecclesiastical footstool. *In order to be properly equipped for Christian discipleship the Christian needs all three legs of the Christian faith.*

Today there is a debate going on in many churches involving the present Pentecostal phenomenon, which is manifesting itself in almost all denominations on a worldwide scale. In view of this, the words of William Law, written in the 1700s, have an eerie quality in their relevance: "A lack of complete submission to the will of God, and a failure to realize that our salvation can only be worked out by the power of the indwelling Holy Spirit forming the very life of Christ within the redeemed heart, has placed the Christian church today in the same apostasy that characterized the Jewish nation. And it has occurred for one and the same reason. The Jews refused Him who was the substance and fulfilling of all that was taught in their Law and Prophets. The Christian church is in a fallen state for the same rejection of the Holy Spirit, who was given to be the power and fulfilling of all that was promised by the Gospel. And just as the Pharisees' rejection of Christ was under a profession of faith in the Messianic Scriptures, so church leaders today reject the demonstration and power of the Holy Spirit in the name of sound doctrine. The Holy Spirit's coming was no less to fulfill the Gospel than Christ's coming was the fulfillment of the Law and the Prophets." The study of earlier Christian writings shows that the problem has never been that God withholds His Spirit from the church or from individuals, but rather that at times the Church and individuals refuse this great gift.

Without opening himself to the power and guidance of the Holy Spirit, a Christian is forced to rely solely on his own natural strength and wisdom. No matter how dedicated and zealous, such a person will eventually wear down. The demands are more than he can meet. If he admits, "Lord, I can't do it," he has taken the first step to opening himself to the power and guidance of the Holy Spirit. The Bible is filled with promises that God will freely give His Holy Spirit to His children. One of the clearest is found in Luke 11:13: "If you then, who are evil, know how to give good gifts to your children, how much more will the heavenly Father give the Holy Spirit to those who ask him!"

The person who accepts Jesus Christ as Lord and Savior is a Christian, but if he stops there he is a nominal, ineffective one. It is much the same as the person who goes through a marriage ceremony. He or she is married, but it is an in-name-only state. It is but the first step of a lifelong commitment.

The Church, as individuals and corporately, must follow personal commitment to Jesus with Bible study as an ongoing program if there is to be growth in the faith. Without this there will be little understanding of the Gospel and little, if any, zeal and enthusiasm for spreading the Good News to others.

Without regular feeding on Holy Communion and participation in the other sacraments, the Christian is undernourished and ill-equipped. The Sacramental leg of the Church emphasizes the belief that God manifests Himself to man in special points of contact, such as the sacraments. Because of this, the physical agents of bread and wine, the water of baptism, and Christian fellowship are infused with a supernatural element that is from God.

Leon Morris writes: "It is still a fact that there are ideas in the Bible that are not 'our own ideas' and that when we go to the Bible humbly and in a spirit of readiness to learn we find them there." It is from Scripture that the need for the sacramental emphasis comes. Paul, in his letter to the Corinthians, writes: "The cup of blessing which we bless, is it not a participation in the blood of Christ? The bread which we break, is it not a participation in the body of Christ?" (1 Corinthians 10:16). Christians through the ages have discovered that participating in the sacrament of Holy Communion has given them a sense of God's immediate presence in their lives. Paul adds, "For I received from the Lord what I also delivered to you, that the Lord Jesus on the night when he was betrayed took bread, and when he had given thanks, he broke it, and said, 'This is my body which is for you. Do this in remembrance of me.' In the same way also the cup, after supper, saying, 'This cup is the new covenant in my blood. Do this, as often as you drink it, in remembrance of me.' For as often as you eat this bread and drink the cup, you proclaim the Lord's death until he comes" (1 Corinthians 11:23–26).

Of the sacrament of baptism, Paul writes: "We were buried therefore with him by baptism into death, so that as Christ was raised from the dead by the glory of the Father, we too might walk in newness of life" (Romans 6:4). Both baptism and Communion are sacraments of new life, instituted by Christ Himself as rites of this new life.

The sacrament of Christian fellowship was seen at the birth of the Christian Church. The disciples and some of the women who had followed Jesus had been waiting together in the Upper Room, and Acts records that *with one accord* they had devoted themselves to prayer. The unity of this Christian fellowship provided the setting for the outpouring of the Holy Spirit. Later, after Peter and John had been arrested for proclaiming Jesus and released, they rejoined the group of followers. "And when they had prayed, the place in which they were gathered together was shaken; and they were all filled with the Holy Spirit and spoke the word of God with boldness" (Acts 4:31). It is impossible to read the New Testament without noticing that when people are together in true Christian fellowship, the Spirit of God is present in great power.

The individual or parish that keeps a balance between the three legs of God's ecclesiastical stool is like a person who is healthy in body, soul, and spirit. Good physical health, a sound mental state, and spiritual well-being are marks of a whole person. Proper emphasis on the Pentecostal, Evangelical, and Sacramental legs of the Christian faith are marks of a whole church.

The result of such wholeness is a state of energy and enthusiasm similar to what has been labeled the "flow experience." A writer for *The Washington Post*, writing in terms of sports, said that the flow experience is that ecstatic feeling when everything is just right—when an athlete has reached his or her full potential and loses sense of time and externals. In the late 1960s the University of Chicago began to study this flow experience. People of various professions were interviewed, and it was found that prestige, reward, and glamour ranked below other factors in why the person did what he or she did. The common denominator among all of those interviewed—and their real reward—was the flow experience. They all sought this "high," an altered state of being that occurred when they were deeply involved in the activity.

There is an element of spirituality in all flow experiences, and the Bible records many specifically religious ones. Moses and the burning bush, Jacob wrestling with the angel, the first disciples at Pentecost, and John on the island of Patmos are some of them.

Mother Teresa gives us a good example of someone in a modern-day flow experience. She is so engrossed in her work among the poor in Calcutta, India, that she seems oblivious to any personal needs. Despite what to most of us in this country are unbearable living conditions, she displays a peace and serenity that can only come from the flow of God's Spirit into her and through her. Since she is a member of one of the Sacramental branches of the Church, is obviously filled with the Holy Spirit, and devotes her life to outreach to the needy in the name of Jesus, she is good evidence of one who operates within a balance of the three legs of God's Church.

All of us can enjoy this flow experience when we surrender ourselves to the Lordship of Jesus Christ, ask for the power of the Holy Spirit to be released in us, open ourselves to fresh infillings, and continue to be nourished and instructed by the Bible and the sacraments. As with the athletes who attain this experience, we need determination and discipline to reach this goal.

NINE

The Sacramental Leg

The Church has always defined a sacrament as an outward and visible form of an inward grace. Using this definition, we recognize Jesus as the first sacrament of the Christian Church. He was the visible, physical expression of God's grace. He literally acted out God's love for mankind through His ministry, death, and resurrection. The Gospels record that throughout His life He was a special point of contact between man and God, and Christians continue to find this true.

We are by nature sacramental people. We need something physical—visible and tangible—to help us connect with the spiritual—the intangible. The giving and receiving of rings during a wedding ceremony are sacraments, in that they express the love and commitment of the couple for each other. Giving a teenager the keys to the family car can be a sacrament, if it expresses the parents' love and trust for the child. Whether we are conscious of it or not, we live our lives using sacraments as special points of contact to express or symbolize our feelings.

The two sacraments that were instituted by Christ as means for receiving God's grace were Christian baptism and

Holy Communion. Scripture teaches that at baptism God adopts us, gives us His Holy Spirit, grafts us into the Body of Christ, makes us members of the New Covenant, and makes us co-inheritors with Christ of the Kingdom of heaven. Baptism is the sacrament of new birth: it represents death and resurrection. The old man dies—"drowns"—and is raised a new creation with a new spirit and a new nature. Of course, God is not limited to the sacraments. He can adopt anyone He chooses and give him all the privileges of rebirth, but in the sacrament of baptism we fulfill Christ's command to be baptized.

In Holy Communion, which is the central act of worship, we receive the body and blood of Jesus for nourishment. This sacrament, sometimes called the Lord's Supper, the Eucharist, the Divine Liturgy, the Mass, or the Great Offering, is the way the sacrifice of Christ is made present. The benefits we receive through the giving and receiving of the bread and wine, according to Christ's command, are the strengthening of our union with Christ and with each other, the forgiveness of our sins, and the promise of the heavenly banquet that awaits us in the next life. In return, we should offer God thanksgiving for all His blessings and offer ourselves to Him for His service. Failure to do this belittles Christ's sacrifice and shows indifference to God's love for us. We need the power of this outward sacrament along with the appropriate inner response in order to make our professed commitment to Christ a living reality in our lives.

I was raised in a denomination where baptism and the Lord's Supper were considered sacraments. The Lord's Supper was celebrated every Sunday, but as a *memorial* meal. It was not until years later that I understood that a sacrament is something through which God acts and man responds. For example, if God does not do something in baptism, all the person does is get wet. If God does not do something in Holy Communion, all the person does is sip wine or grape juice and taste bread or a wafer. What makes a sacrament effective and power-filled is God's action and man's cooperation.

I was baptized when I was twelve years old because all the others in my Sunday school class were being baptized. I had no idea what baptism really meant. All it meant to me was that I would be included in the goings-on that were going on.

Ten years later, Anne and I were married. I was the manager of a movie theatre, and three months after our marriage I was transferred to another state to manage a theatre there. Anne and I wanted to attend church together, and as she was a cradle Episcopalian, I decided to join that church. The bishop was coming for confirmation in three weeks so I was invited to be confirmed, in spite of having had no instructions about the beliefs of the Episcopal Church. My confirmation, like my baptism, meant nothing to me—but it did to God. He is always faithful to do what He promises and whenever we begin to cooperate, changes take place in our lives.

I believe that I received the Holy Spirit when I was baptized, just as I believe all who are baptized receive Him. I believe that He began a work in me that eventually led me to confirmation, which is intended to be a lesser sacrament in which the person reaffirms his baptismal vows and the power of the Spirit is released in him. Even though I did not know or understand what was happening at the time, I know now that it was the Holy Spirit who was urging and nudging me into a deeper commitment to Jesus Christ as my Lord, as well as my Savior. Regularly receiving Holy Communion helped, even when I did not understand its meaning or its benefits.

Anne and I continued to attend church and as our five children were born, attended Sunday school as well. We were fortunate to have a pastor who was a good preacher and excellent teacher. We learned more about the Bible, and became interested in learning more about the Christian faith. We read books and attended conferences while becoming more and more involved in the Christian fellowship of our parish. Finally, thirteen years after my confirmation, I was convinced that God was calling me to go from being an active layman to the ordained ministry, and I started college as a freshman with that goal in mind. I am positive that it was the work of the Holy Spirit, combined with my cooperation, that led me into the priesthood.

During the years that I was working toward my college degree, some friends sent us a Christmas card with "Philippians 1:3–6" written in the margin. When we looked this up, we read: "I thank my God in all my remembrance of you, always in every prayer of mine for you all making my prayer with joy, thankful for your partnership in the gospel from the first day until now. And I am sure that he who began a good work in you will bring it to completion at the day of Jesus Christ."

I include this story because it illustrates two points: It is an example of the sacrament of Christian fellowship, which can take form in Christian friendship as well as in larger groups, and it reminds us that God is faithful to finish what He starts, which is very reassuring when we apply this to our own Christian growth.

During the ten years that I was rector at St. Bartholomew's Episcopal Church in Nashville, Tennessee, we celebrated Holy Communion every morning, Monday through Friday, at 6:15 A.M. This was in addition to the regular Sunday Eucharists, a midweek Communion with unction for the sick, and a Saturday morning service.

The early morning Communion services were very special. An average of twenty to thirty people attended, some every day, others less frequently. Following the service, we all met together for breakfast, Bible reading, prayers, and sharing. In this daily coming together, we experienced the presence of God in both the sacrament of Holy Communion and the sacrament of Christian fellowship. Gradually, we came to realize that we were repeating the custom of the early Church described in Acts 2:42, as we devoted ourselves to the apostles' teaching through reading from the Bible and other devotional books, to fellowship through sharing our lives with each other, to the breaking of bread in both Communion and shared breakfasts, and to the prayers. One of the members of this group referred to it as "the praying heart of the church," because intercessory prayers were such a vital part of this group.

Although baptism and Holy Communion are the primary sacraments, others are important also if we are to be properly equipped for the life and ministry that Christ has called us to. In most of the sacraments a vow is made, and the person making it needs the power of God in order to keep it.

Confirmation is the rite in which we express a mature commitment to Christ, and receive the infilling of the Holy Spirit through the laying on of hands. This practice has its roots in the Old Testament, when Elijah lay his hands on Elisha, for instance, as the transference of power and authority. It also has roots in the New Testament when converts received the laying on of hands for the release of the Holy Spirit in them. An example of this is found in Acts 8:14–17 when Peter and John went to Samaria to pray for converts who had been baptized but had not received the release of the Spirit in their lives. In a very real sense, confirmation should be recognized as "ordination to the lay ministry," as this is the time the Christian is empowered for the service of Christ. Although we receive the Holy Spirit at baptism or whenever we accept Jesus as our Savior, the power of the Spirit must be released in us if we are to live the new life and fulfill our God-given ministry. This power can be released in us anytime we ask for it to be, but the rite of confirmation sets aside a particular time and place for asking. Unfortunately, confirmation is thought of by some as the time they join a particular denomination or, for young people, as graduation from Sunday school. In reality, it is intended to be a new beginning: a deeper walk with the Lord and the acceptance of a ministry to others in His name.

In the sacrament of holy matrimony, the couple make their vows to each other, and ask God to be a partner in their life together. They vow before God and the church to enter into a lifelong union, and in this sacrament they receive the grace and blessing of God to aid them in fulfilling this vow.

In the sacrament of holy unction, or healing, God's healing power is released through the anointing with oil and the laying on of hands. As in all the sacraments, God's power is not limited to the particular action, but it is a special way in which He works. This sacrament does not necessarily involve a vow from the recipient, although one may be included.

Healing is often blocked because of unresolved guilt, resentment, or unforgiveness. That is why the sacrament of penance, or confession and absolution, sometimes should precede the sacrament of holy unction. In the sacrament of penance a vow is not necessarily spoken, but it is understood that the person is truly penitent and intends to lead a new life. It is impossible for this intention to become a reality without help from almighty God. In the sacrament of penance, the person confesses his sins and failures, and God provides His forgiveness. Although forgiveness is available when sin and failure are confessed, it is important that the person believes that he is forgiven, that God has wiped the slate clean.

Many people find it hard to accept forgiveness from God, but they sometimes find it even harder to forgive themselves. It is important to our emotional health that we confess our sins, and then accept God's forgiveness. Guilt—real or imagined—is one of the heaviest burdens a person can bear. Furthermore, resentment and the refusal to forgive others can not only block healing, it can *cause* physical illness. If more people confessed their sins, released their guilt, and accepted God's forgiveness, there would be fewer ulcers, headaches, and arthritic pain. Obviously, not every instance of these maladies is due to the feeling of being unforgiven, but I believe many of them are. I do not support compulsory confession, nor do I think it is necessary to confess to a priest, but it seems that, sometimes, just confessing to God does not relieve the burden of guilt that we may feel inside. There is something healing about confessing to another person. Again, this does not have to be in formal ritual—it may be in a conversational manner. But I feel sure that Christians would be healthier emotionally and physically if we took advantage of the benefits of confession. Incidentally, it should be understood that the priest does not forgive you. What he does is pronounce *God's* forgiveness of you. His personal feelings have no bearing on the efficacy of this sacrament.

A final sacrament is the one of Holy Orders. This is for the beginning of the ordained ministry. In this service the person makes vows and it is only with God's help that those vows can be kept. The "laying on of hands" in this sacrament is another channel through which God's power is infused and released in the newly ordained person. *A denomination gives the authority for a person to be an ordained minister, but God is the only one who can give the power.*

I am a great believer in the efficacy of the sacraments, but I am just as aware that they are not enough in themselves. There must be a personal commitment to Jesus Christ on our part, there must be a study of God's Word, and we must open ourselves to the Holy Spirit so that we will receive a zeal and power to bring others into the Kingdom under the

Lordship of Jesus Christ. There is a vital, all-important need to have the Holy Spirit's power released in us if we are to experience personally the blessings of the Kingdom here on earth.

As we become more aware of a sacrament as "an outward and visible sign of an inward and spiritual grace, given by Christ as sure and certain means by which we receive that grace" (*The Book of Common Prayer*), we can often recognize the sacramental nature of some of the events and occasions of our ordinary experiences. This was demonstrated by Jesus when He used the familiar Passover meal to institute the sacrament of Holy Communion in which ordinary bread and wine of the Jewish meal could be experienced as the living presence of the Lord—His body and blood.

Thanksgiving or Christmas dinners have become sacramental in nature for many people. The gathering of the family, often from some distance, is the outward expression of the inward love and ties among the participants. Many times a person who says grace for the food also expresses thanks for the family and perhaps asks God's continuing presence and blessings for those present.

Sacraments are not limited to events such as meals or family reunions. They can also be recognized in behavior. A smile or hug can be a sacrament. Through them, love, sympathy, friendship, or concern can be communicated. Even the most hardened cynic usually responds to the guileless smile of a baby or young child, because it expresses an innocence and good humor that belie current headlines of hopelessness. Many times, especially as an expression of sympathy, a hug is better than words for saying, "I'm sorry. I care and I am here if you need me." Parents learn early that a hug can soothe a crying child, and later that hugs may be better than words for communicating, "I love you. Be careful. Come back safely" all the many times we send our children out into the world of school, dates, jobs, or adventure.

Sacraments communicate grace and love and help us keep life in balance by reminding us of the relationship between the physical and spiritual in our lives. They remind us that all things become holy when they are held up to God, set apart for God, or offered to Him for His use. Countless parents have found strength and comfort in remembering that their children are gifts from God. By entrusting them to Him they are participating in a sacrament that may be expressed through releasing them from the bondage of parental apron strings. If we deliberately look for signs of the sacramental in the affairs of our everyday lives, we are inevitably brought full circle back into the need for the Church's sacraments. We desperately need the strengthening of the sacraments in order to free each other from bondage, and to live victoriously in this world.

It is important to remember that a sacrament is something that God does, but for it to be effective we must cooperate with it and participate in it. Working in tandem, God's power and our obedience become a powerful force for making the Kingdom of God visible in the world.

To deny, ignore, or neglect the Sacramental leg on which the Church stands is to greatly restrict the effectiveness and spiritual health of the members of the Church, and the corporate Body of Christ.

TEN

The Pentecostal Leg

The Pentecostal leg takes its name from the outpouring of the Holy Spirit at Pentecost, which is celebrated as the birthday of the Christian Church. The Holy Spirit, or third Person of God, however, has always been present in the world and active in the lives of men and women. In fact, the Bible opens with the statement that before the earth took shape or light dawned, the Spirit of God was moving over the face of the waters.

Early on the Hebrews saw evidence of the Spirit in people with special gifts and abilities. The book of Exodus speaks of Bezalel as being filled by the Spirit of God with ability, intelligence, knowledge, and all craftsmanship. Deuteronomy tells of Joshua being filled with the spirit of wisdom. Judges attributes the great strength of Samson to the fact that the Spirit of the Lord came mightily upon him. In particular, the Jews felt that the Spirit was given to those appointed to communicate the will of God to His people. Isaiah 61 opens with the words, "The Spirit of the Lord God is upon me, because the Lord has anointed me to bring good tidings to the afflicted . . . to proclaim the year of the Lord's favor."

We in the latter part of this century are blessed to be enjoying a fresh outpouring of the Holy Spirit. This has been labeled by some as the charismatic renewal. The dictionary defines charismatic as having charisma—*charismata* is Greek for gifts—and charisma is defined as favor, grace, or having a special gift of leadership. Actually, this is not a very good term to describe the present activity of the Holy Spirit, but at least it denotes that there is something special going on today. Richard Quebedeaux, in his book *The New Charismatics*, explains this with the statement, "In a word, Charismatic Renewal is a celebration in our generation that God has not forgotten His promises, that He is, in fact and deed, a living God, totally committed to work in *evidential* ways through the lives of those committed to Him."

The Holy Spirit is the living, always contemporary personality who offers fresh revelations of the mind of God. The book of Revelation, in the final chapter, states: "The Spirit and the Bride say, 'Come.' And let him who . . . is thirsty come, let him who desires take the water of life without price" (Revelation 22:17). The Spirit continually invites us all to come to Jesus, to drink the water of life that He offers, and to be made new—to come alive. This is why the Nicene Creed describes the Holy Spirit as "the Lord, Giver of Life."

The Pentecostal leg emphasizes that it is the activity of the Holy Spirit that makes our faith real to us. The Holy Spirit acts in our lives in ways that we can recognize to point us to the presence of Jesus and the love and grace of the Father toward us. Without the Holy Spirit acting in and on our lives, the faith we profess often seems dry and dull—perhaps even dead. Church attendance is a duty rather than a joy. Prayer, if we pray, is a ritual that gives no feeling of the nearness of God and offers us little hope of any changes in our situation. Bible study is avoided because it seems arid and irrelevant to our lives.

Jesus made it very clear that when He returned to the Father the disciples would need help, and He would provide it. "I will not leave you desolate; I will come to you," He promised (John 14:18). A little later He says to them: "These things I have spoken to you, while I am still with you. But the Counselor, the Holy Spirit, whom the Father will send in my name, he will teach you all things, and bring to your remembrance all that I have said to you. Peace I leave with you; my peace I give to you; not as the world gives do I give to you. Let not your hearts be troubled, neither let them be afraid" (John 14:25–27).

In these words we find a list of some of the functions of the Holy Spirit: He points us to Jesus; He teaches us; He opens the Scriptures to us in ways that we can understand and apply to our lives; He reveals new truths to us through people or events; He "brings to our remembrance," that is, He reminds us over and over, of times that we have been conscious of God at work in our lives, whether deliverance from problems, protection from dangers, or simply an experience of the peace that Jesus promised.

We need evidence of the presence and power of God that comes through the Holy Spirit. We are physical people and we often need specific physical events to assure us of God's personal concern for us.

Anne and I were particularly conscious of the Holy Spirit's presence in our lives during our three years at seminary. We were provided with free housing through a committed Christian judge who offered a house for some seminary family to use. Financial gifts came to us from various people who were aware of the expenses a family of seven faced in the Washington, D.C., area. Our family discovered what true togetherness is in a house with five rooms and one bath. But we all have happy memories of those years in Virginia. Looking back on this experience reminds us often that God always provides for our needs, and that the Holy Spirit's presence transforms our circumstances as well as our attitudes.

It is the strategy of those "principalities and powers" that St. Paul warns about to try and keep us from remembering God. If this happens, we are unplugged from our source of life and power. We are disconnected—very much as if we were cut off during a phone conversation. The Holy Spirit is the "operator" who reconnects us to the presence of God.

Henri J. M. Nouwen, author and respected theologian, writes of this need for the remembrance of God in his book *The Living Reminder.* He says that there is a vital need in Christian ministry for the conviction that "nothing, absolutely nothing, in our lives is outside the realm of God's judgment and mercy. By hiding parts of our story, not only from our own consciousness but also from God's eye, we claim a divine role for ourselves: we become judges of our own past and limit mercy to our own fears."

Nothing is more bleak or terrifying than to be cut off from the memory of God. When we let Him, the Holy Spirit will gently and lovingly show us that God has been present in all that has happened to us, even those events that seem at the time most painful.

The Holy Spirit always points to Jesus, which means that through Him we are constantly reminded that God accepts us and approves of us simply because we have accepted Jesus as our Savior. John V. Taylor, in *The Go-Between God,* expressed this as he wrote of "my painfully reluctant realization that my Father is not going to be any more pleased with me when I am good than he is now when I am bad. He accepts me and delights in me as I am. It is ridiculous of him, but that is how it is between us. In consequence, I want to show my love for him fully and continuously, and I can do that best by insisting on my freedom to push into his presence, grubby and outrageous, without having first to wash my hands and comb my hair. Once we have grasped this . . . that God loves us for ourselves as we are and has accepted us because of Jesus and not because we have become good, two things are bound to follow. First, we begin to trust the warmth and spontaneity of love and to welcome the gift of love in all the varied forms and experiences in which it comes to us . . . and second, we turn into basically accepting people." To know, deep inside, that God accepts me and delights in me just as I am is to know a joy and freedom from guilt that cannot be described.

The gift of the Holy Spirit makes Jesus real to us and reveals Him as the Anointed One of God. It is the Holy Spirit who assures us that we belong to God. The Holy Spirit is given to inspire us—to make us "alive" and able to experience life in the Kingdom of God on earth. But He is also given to equip us for ministry. He is present at conversion, because "no one can say 'Jesus is Lord' except by the Holy Spirit" (1 Corinthians 12:3), but He is also the one who helps us go on to the next step: from conversion to ministry; from new birth to new life.

The various gifts of the Holy Spirit equip us for this ministry. Ephesians 4:7–8, 11–12 says: "But grace was given to each of us according to the measure of Christ's gift. Therefore it is said, 'When he ascended on high he led a host of captives, and he gave gifts to men.' . . . And his gifts were that some should be apostles, some prophets, some evangelists, some pastors and teachers, *for the equipment of the saints, for the work of ministry, for building up the body of Christ.*" To equip Christians for ministry in order to build up the Church is the reason for the various gifts of the Holy Spirit. Some of those gifts such as wisdom, knowledge, faith, healing power, miracle working, prophecy, discernment, tongues, and the interpretation of tongues are listed in 1 Corinthians 12. Other gifts are listed in the twelfth chapter of Romans and other places in the Bible. The Holy Spirit's

gifts are often supernatural gifts, but at other times He en-
hances our natural gifts and talents. All of them are to be
used to the glory of God and to build up—numerically and
spiritually—the Body of Christ.

Many people do not understand just what the phrase
"fully God and fully man" means when it is used in describing Jesus. Some think of Him as a great prophet,
teacher, and leader, but deny His divinity by overempha-
sizing His humanity. Others think of Him more as God
walking around pretending to be a man, and so deny His
humanity. It is essential for us to understand both His humanity and His divinity if we are to appreciate the magni-
tude of the Christ Event and also in order to have a better
understanding of the working of the Holy Spirit.

When the Christ, the Son of God, the second Person of
the Trinity, came to earth in the form of Jesus of Nazareth,
He deliberately chose to limit Himself to the dimensions of
a first-century Jew. He was not just walking around pretending to be a man; He was a first-century Jew with the
knowledge and understanding of a first-century Jew. He
thought the world was three-layered: hell, earth, and
heaven. He knew nothing of penicillin, computers, or many
things familiar to us in the twentieth century. He did have a
better insight into the nature of God and the nature of man
and the relationship between the two, but He chose to limit
Himself to being a man of His century. Neither history nor
the Bible records anything that might be considered spec-
tacular or supernatural about the first thirty years of his life.
I realize that you may be saying to yourself, "What about
the incident in the Temple when He was twelve?" Actually,
all good Jewish boys should have been "about their Father's
business"—preparing for their Bar Mitzvah, talking to and
learning from the religious leaders. There was nothing necessarily unusual about His being in the Temple then. Nothing of a nature that would give an inkling of who He was

The Pentecostal Leg

and why He was in the world occurred until His baptism in the River Jordan by John the Baptist.

No devout Christian can question the fact that Jesus "had" the Holy Spirit from the moment of His conception; He was conceived by the Holy Spirit. That is a basic tenet of the Christian faith. The point that so many people misunderstand is that it was not until He was baptized that the power of the Spirit was *released* in Him. From that moment on He was able to perform miracles, teach with divine inspiration, and lay the groundwork for the universal mission and ministry of the Church.

This idea of the release of the Spirit in Jesus' life can irritate those who only see Him as a great teacher and example, and offend those who only see Him as God pretending to be a man. Nevertheless, Scripture attests to the fact that although He was fully divine, He was also fully human, and it was not until His baptism, a "human" gesture, that divine power was released in His life.

Some Christians carry a misperception of the divine/human relationship a step beyond Jesus' life into the lives of the disciples. They expect to see evidence of the Spirit's power in Jesus' life, but hesitate to expect that same power in their own lives. But since we know from the Bible that the disciples exhibited the outpouring of the Holy Spirit in the same way Jesus did, they conclude that the disciples were supermen, superior human agents in a different class from us ordinary mortals. Quite simply, they were not.

The disciples were ordinary people, as weak and sinful as anyone else. Judas betrayed Jesus, Peter denied Him three times, and all of the others, with the possible exception of John, deserted Him. They never really understood what He was talking about the whole time He was with them. They did not have the gifts of wisdom, knowledge, understanding, and discernment—the divine gifts that Jesus exhibited—until they received the Holy Spirit the night of the resurrec-

105

tion and the subsequent release of power at Pentecost. "On the evening of that day, the first day of the week, the doors being shut where the disciples were, for fear of the Jews, Jesus came and stood among them and said to them, 'Peace be with you.' When he had said this, he showed them his hands and his side. Then the disciples were glad when they saw the Lord. Jesus said to them again, 'Peace be with you. As the Father has sent me, even so I send you.' And when he had said this, he breathed on them, and said to them, 'Receive the Holy Spirit' " (John 20:19–22). Luke 24:49 adds: "And behold, I send the promise of my Father upon you; but stay in the city, until you are clothed with power from on high." Then, on the day of Pentecost, "a sound came from heaven like the rush of a mighty wind, and it filled all the house where they were sitting. . . . And they were all filled with the Holy Spirit" (Acts 2:2, 4).

From that time on, those cowards became heroes. They were able to continue victoriously to carry on the ministry and mission of Jesus Christ and change the world.

Just as it is puzzling to think of Jesus' needing the Spirit's empowerment before He could fulfill what He came to earth to do, and hard to think of the disciples as ordinary, Spirit-empowered people, it is even more difficult to get many Christians to understand that if they have accepted Jesus as their Savior, they too have received the Holy Spirit and have access to the same power and authority.

Peter, James, John, and all of the rest of the disciples did not receive one bit more than all Christians have received; the difference comes in their openness to the release of the Spirit's power. The power is available in our lives, but there must come a time when it is released if we are to do and be what we are called to do and be. Then we, ordinary people that we are, will find miraculously that we can join Jesus in this release of spiritual power in the midst of our humanity. This, of course, does not mean we share in His divinity, but it does mean that we can have the power of the Spirit working through us as He did, and can have the assurance that we belong to God. We might think of the Holy Spirit as a down payment on the full inheritance that is to be ours as adopted children of God.

We must never think His presence means that we are wonderful people and deserve such rewards. His gifts are given for the purpose of ministering to others in the name of Jesus. They help us in our witness to the resurrection of our Lord, and as a result of this renewed ministry, we will find that the gifts and the power are being manifested in more and more churches. The Holy Spirit can blow on the embers of a seemingly dead Church and bring forth flames of renewal.

I have seen churches all over America and in other parts of the world where this is happening. The gifts of the Holy Spirit are being claimed, received, and used in ministry for the glory of God. Lives are completely changed and enriched. Parents and children are reconciled, marriages are healed, physical healings occur, and in these churches there is a spirit of love and acceptance that is evident to members and visitors alike.

An example of the way the gifts of the Spirit are intended for ministry and for building up the Body of Christ was seen in our own lives two years ago.

Anne and I had been praying for some time for discernment as to whether I should remain at St. Bartholomew's as rector or resign to do full-time teaching missions. We had not shared this concern with our congregation as we felt it would be best to pray it through alone.

One Sunday during the worship service the Lord gave a message to a young lawyer in the congregation and told him it was meant for Anne and me. The young man knew about the gifts of the Spirit, but he didn't expect God to speak through him, he told us later, so he struggled through most of the service trying to decide what to do. Finally he prayed, "Lord, if this is really a message from You, let Anne come up to me after the service and say she needs to talk to me. If this happens, I'll give her the message."

Shortly after praying this prayer, he went to the altar rail to receive Communion. Anne saw him and got an immediate feeling of urgency to talk to him. When the worship service was over she looked for him, but couldn't find him. The feeling that she must talk to him was so strong that she went over to the parish hall to look for him and finally spotted him off in a corner behind a book rack. He admitted later that he was hiding. Anne walked up to him, smiled, and said, "I have to talk to you."

The man hesitated briefly, then launched into a description of what had happened in church and gave a long message to the effect that Anne and I were to begin classes in that church on the Kingdom of heaven and would later go into the world with the same message. Anne copied as much of it as she could on her church bulletin for fear she would forget some of it. Later, when we recovered from the shock of this experience, we began to study and teach on the Kingdom, as instructed. After a few months, another friend came to us with a message she said was surely from God because she was one of Anne's best friends and would never think up such a message herself. It was that our time serving at that church was finished, and that we were to go out into mission work on a full-time basis.

When I presented these things to my vestry they accepted them as from the Lord and voted to back us in this ministry with prayer and financial support for as long as it was needed.

Several months later, while doing a mission in upstate New York, we were confronted by a woman who said she felt the Lord was giving her a message in tongues for us and wanted to give it to us. We told her to go ahead. Neither of us got an interpretation, but the rector of that church did. When he interpreted the message it was almost word for word and phrase for phrase what the lawyer had told us months before. The chief difference was that it began at the point that instructed we were to go out from our parish, and added a few lines to the effect that we were not to be anxious because we were in God's will for us. All we could say was, "Praise God!"

Several gifts of the Holy Spirit were manifested through these events. The message the lawyer received was prophecy. Wisdom was necessary as we sought guidance through prayer and the advice of the vestry. Tongues and interpretation of tongues were given to confirm the message and our response to it.

It is through the Pentecostal leg that the power of the Holy Spirit is employed. To neglect this leg is to attempt to fulfill the commission from Christ unequipped; it means trying to perform an impossible task in our own strength and wisdom.

Just before Jesus ascended to the Father the disciples asked Him, " 'Lord, will you at this time restore the kingdom to Israel?' He said to them, 'It is not for you to know times or seasons which the Father has fixed by his own authority. But you shall receive power when the Holy Spirit has come upon you; and you shall be my witnesses in Jerusalem and in all Judea and Samaria and to the end of the earth' " (Acts 1:6–8).

The Holy Spirit is still the source of the power we need in order to be the Body of Christ on earth. The Church simply cannot fulfill her mission without Him.

ELEVEN

The Evangelical Leg

The Evangelical leg of the Church emphasizes the Bible, personal commitment to Jesus, and the need for outreach to others in His name. It must grieve the heart of God that after almost two thousand years, Christians are just a small minority in the world. This is true partly because so many people who sit in church pews on Sunday are still mission fields. *Everybody in the world is either a missionary or a mission field.* It is the missionaries who are proclaiming the good news of Jesus Christ and spreading the Gospel by word and deed.

I don't think that the majority of Christians know the promises or the responsibilities that are stated in God's Word. They don't know what God expects of them so they settle for going to church on Sunday and trying to be "good." Many do not know what their own denomination believes or teaches. The lack of Bible teaching in many parishes, and the failure of church members to read and study the Bible at home, creates ignorant—not stupid—but ignorant Christians. Uninformed Christians are ineffective Christians. Uninformed, and therefore uncommitted, these Christians remain mission fields.

When a person makes a personal commitment of his life to Jesus Christ, receives sound Bible teaching, understands that Jesus has called and commissioned him, and the Holy Spirit has equipped him, he inevitably becomes a missionary to others. Some may feel called to a foreign mission field, but others realize that much of the "Christian" world is ripe for harvest. Out of gratitude to God for saving him *from* the things that blight his life and saving him *for* all the blessings of the Kingdom of God on earth and beyond, he is consumed with a passion to tell others the good news of Jesus Christ.

One of the definitions of the word *evangel* is "glad tidings." If we think of the Evangelical leg of God's Church in light of this definition, it is easy to see why it is so important. Gospel means good news and it will remain good news as we enjoy life in the Kingdom and try to recruit others to come into this Kingdom under the Lordship of Jesus Christ.

Serving the Lord is not drudgery but joy. The evangelical emphasis on the need for Bible study and the need for witnessing to others about Christ—what He has done, is doing, and will do—points to two of the avenues that Christians discover they must follow if they are to experience their own glad tidings.

When the Bible is neglected there are no guidelines for living except our own feelings or ideas. When we never speak of our faith to others and live as though being a Christian should be like belonging to some secret organization, we soon discover that our faith is ebbing away. "Closet Christians" do not enjoy the blessings Christ offers, nor do they bring glory to God and blessings to others.

There is a short line in the book of Samuel that was used to describe a time when people were drifting away from God, parents were failing to restrain their children, and there was general apathy among the people. "And the word of the Lord was rare in those days; there was no frequent vision" (1 Samuel 3:1). Whenever the word of the Lord is rare—and this happens when there is no contact with God's Word through Scripture study and worship—there will be no "frequent vision."

The most pathetic people I have ever known have been those who have no vision for life. They are like ships adrift, with no purpose or goal. This is not what God wants for His people. The Bible is the love story of God for man and through it we can find direction for our lives. As God's "manual for living" it is as fresh and relevant as when it was written. This is not surprising, for if God created a world that included creatures made in His image and then gave His Son to bring them out of their rebellion and back into a relationship with Himself, He surely wants us to have a record of this activity. And the Bible is much more than just a record; God still speaks to man through it.

Emil Brunner has called the Bible "his Master's voice" because it is a living record of God's Word to us. It deals with every area of life, and through it we can catch the vision of God in everything we do, every person we meet, and every thought and emotion. The Bible teaches that God can and does communicate with man, and that man can and should respond to Him.

Jesus Christ has given His Church the responsibility and the privilege of sharing His mission and ministry to the world. This is the message and emphasis of the Evangelical leg of the Church. The Bible shows that there are many ways of carrying out Christ's commission, and there is no one pattern that everyone must follow.

If a movie is ever made solely about the disciples, undoubtedly the star roles would be those of Peter, James, and John. These three were the stars of the group, the "inner circle." They were present when Jesus healed Jairus' daughter, was transfigured before them on the Mount, and underwent temptation in the Garden of Gethsemane. These three are perhaps the best known and best loved of the disciples. They, along with Paul, seem to be the favorites of the clergy. Yet there are two lesser disciples, Andrew and Philip, whom we should study as examples of evangelists. Their slogan was "come and see."

One day Andrew and a friend, then disciples of John the Baptist, were following Jesus at a distance out of curiosity. Jesus turned and asked the most fundamental question in a person's life: "What are you looking for?" By way of an answer they asked, "Where are you staying?" They probably hoped to spend time with Him and discuss their problems and questions about life. When Jesus said to them, "Come and see," He was inviting them not only to come and talk, but to find the things that He alone could open to them. They came and stayed with Jesus the rest of the day. Then Andrew returned to his brother Peter with the news, "We have found the Messiah," and brought him to Jesus. (See John 1:37–42.)

What little we know about Andrew paints him as one of the most attractive of the disciples, yet he was always willing to take second place. Although he lived in his brother's shadow, all that mattered to him was to be with Jesus and serve Him any way he could. Andrew had a missionary's heart and is an example of one who could not keep Jesus to himself.

Philip was another who brought others to Jesus. He told his friend Nathanael that he had found the long-promised Messiah in Jesus of Nazareth. Nathanael's reaction was, "Can anything good come out of Nazareth?" Philip was wise enough not to argue. He simply said, "Come and see." One cannot argue someone into believing. Conversion is the work of the Holy Spirit; our call is to invite others to come and see.

It is not enough to proclaim the Gospel or witness about

our faith to others. There must be follow-up for any who accept the invitation to come and see. They must be nurtured by regular attendance at worship services, fellowship with other Christians, and participation in Bible study, prayer groups, and courses on the Christian faith. One-time commitment will not last unless the person becomes involved in the life, worship, and work of Christ's Body.

We may not be great preachers like Peter, or great teachers like Paul, but everyone can be a witness and recruiter for Christ. Even the shut-in can minister and recruit by telephone and letter. If we are willing to obey our Lord's command to reach out to others, He will send people to us who are hungry to hear the message.

The Christian faith cannot be clutched to oneself. A relationship with Jesus is not something we can have exclusively. When we let Jesus into our lives, He insists on bringing His other friends with Him. The Christian faith must be shared. But many church people would rather fail the one they call their Lord than risk being rejected by their acquaintances or be considered a religious fanatic by their friends. (A good definition of a fanatic is anyone who is willing to go one step further than I am.)

Uninvolved, uncommitted Christians neither harvest the fields nor nurture the new Christians that others bring in. Knowing Jesus should make us burn with the desire to introduce Him to others. Being spiritually fed ourselves should make us want to invite others to the banquet. There is a saying that makes this point: Evangelism is one beggar telling another beggar where to find food.

If we are not in a personal relationship with Jesus, if we have not found something that has changed our lives, and if we are not being fed spiritually, we must ask ourselves the question, "Am I still a mission field?" If the Christian proclamation seems like "religious talk" to us, if we are still hurting or bitter from experiences in our lives, and if we are not experiencing the peace and joy that Jesus offers, then the answer is probably yes.

If this is the case, I urge you to "hie thee" to a Christian church that preaches Jesus, teaches the Bible, and is open to all the Holy Spirit offers. There will be someone there—the minister or some lay people—who will talk to you and proclaim the good news to you, and show you how to avail yourself of all Christ wants you to have. Please take advantage of this.

If you are not a mission field but wonder if you are a missionary, I urge you to take seriously St. Paul's admonition in his second letter to Timothy: "Do your best to present yourself to God as one approved, a workman who has no need to be ashamed, rightly handling the word of truth" (2:15). Through Jesus, we *are* approved. The only shame we need ever feel is that we fail to carry out the work God has given us to do.

The work of the Church is: *Proclaiming* the good news; *witnessing* to the life-changing power of Jesus Christ in our personal lives; *recruiting* others to come into the Kingdom; and *ministering* to people in Christ's name, while training and nurturing "baby Christians" for these same tasks.

The responsibility for this belongs to the whole Church—both laity and clergy.

The Church has not been as effective as it could and should be because many times the members feel that it is the minister's job to minister and the congregation's job to congregate. If Christianity is to change and influence the world, all of the members must understand that they are called to serve as well as to worship.

The Church is not a spiritual filling station where we go to get tanked up as needed. We are called to come to Jesus, and then go out to the world. The Christian life is a constant coming in and going out. We come in for nourishment and empowerment, and we go out to evangelize, recruit, and minister.

There is an old story about Desert Pete and a sermon he wrote that illustrates the importance of sharing the living water with others. The message had been written with a stub of a pencil on brown wrapping paper that had been folded and placed for protection in a tin baking powder can. The can had been wired to an old pump that offered the only chance of water on a very long, seldom-used trail across the Amargosa Desert. He wrote: "This pump is all right as of June 1932. I put a new sucker-washer into it and it ought to last five years, but the washer dries out and the pump has got to be primed. Under the white rock I buried a bottle of water, out of the sun, the cork end up. There is enough water in it to prime this pump, but not if you drink some first. Pour about one fourth and let her soak to wet the leather. Then pour in the rest medium fast, and pump like the dickens. You'll get water. The well has never run dry. Have faith! When you git watered up, fill the bottle and put it back like you found it for the next feller. Signed, Desert Pete. P.S. Don't go drinking the water first. Prime the pump with it and you'll get all you can hold. And the next time you pray, remember that God is like this pump. He has to be primed. I've given my last dime away a dozen times to prime the pump of my prayers, and I've fed my last beans to a stranger while a-saying 'Amen.' It never failed yet to git me an answer. You got to git your heart fixed to give before you can be give to. Pete."

Like Pete, we need to share what we receive. If we try only to quench our own thirst we become a dry well.

Once on one of those spring days when the country switches over from regular time to Daylight Savings time, a woman who had forgotten to change her clocks arrived at church just as the last hymn was being sung. She asked an usher if the service was over, and he replied, "No! The worship is over, and now it is time for the service to begin." This man clearly understood the purpose of the Evangelical leg of the Church.

The Marks
of a
Healthy Church

How can a person judge the spiritual health of a church? Many dead or dying churches have quite a bit of activity, but it is the *kind* of activity that determines the degree of "life" that is there: Obedience to Christ's command to love and a zeal to fulfill His commission are the only gauges that accurately indicates the spiritual health of a church.

Any size church in any size town that utilizes all three legs that God has provided for His Church can be assured of good health and continued growth. Just as the human body has a built-in ability to grow and heal itself, given the proper conditions, so has the Church. When there is a balance between the Sacramental, Pentecostal, and Evangelical legs, the proper conditions for healthy church life are present.

The five marks of a healthy parish are:

1. *Jesus Christ is allowed to be Lord.*

This may seem to be stating the obvious in reference to a Christian church; nevertheless, in many churches this does not seem to be the case. Where He is indeed allowed to be

Lord, everyone from the leaders of the various organizations down to the individual members always hold before them the question: "What would Jesus have us do?"

This means in practical terms that Jesus is faithfully proclaimed from the pulpit as the Son of God and the Lord of His Church. It means that the individual members not only have accepted Him as their personal Savior, but want Him to be the Lord of their lives—and are trying to live accordingly. They turn to Him in prayer regularly, depend on Him in times of need, and try to follow His teachings in all areas of their lives. As part of their obedience they partake of the sacraments that he instituted, and in so doing discover that He really does meet them there. As opportunities arise, they witness to one another and to those outside the fellowship of the blessings they enjoy because of their relationship with God through Jesus Christ and His Church. Their witness does not have to be dramatic or unusual, but they know that sharing such commonplace happenings as the healing of a fever or getting a better job can build the faith of both the speaker and the hearer. They take seriously Jesus' words to care for widows and orphans. In this area it is encouraging to notice that more and more churches are becoming involved in ministry to the needy. They are doing things such as opening soup kitchens, organizing pantries of food for needy families, and running day care centers for the children of working parents. Involvement in prison ministries, both to the prisoners and to their families, is also beginning or increasing among church members.

It is not surprising that a church that truly allows Jesus to be its Head will care for those in need. Jesus, who is God's love personified, is bound to direct His Body to extend this love to the world in ways the world can recognize. "I was hungry and you gave me food, I was thirsty and you gave me drink. I was a stranger and you welcomed me, I was naked and you clothed me, I was sick and you visited me, I was in prison and you came to me. . . . Truly, I say to you, as you did it to one of the least of these my brethren, you did it to me" (Matthew 25:35–36, 40).

Jesus also said, "And I, when I am lifted up from the earth, will draw all men to myself" (John 12:32). He was lifted up on a Cross, and it is that Cross that does draw people to Him. Today when action follows our profession of faith in Him we are "lifting" Him up, and like a magnet, people are attracted to Him. When Jesus is exalted and obeyed in a parish, the parish inevitably grows—spiritually, numerically, and financially.

2. *The Bible is preached and taught.*

The March 1984 Gallup Poll reported that eight in ten Americans claim to be Christians, but only half know who delivered the Sermon on the Mount, and the majority cannot list even five of the Ten Commandments. This poll also reported that Americans watch an average of six hours of television a day, and two-thirds of them say it is their primary source of information. A third of all adults suffer from persistent feelings of low self-worth. The poll concluded with a quote from columnist Michael J. McManus: "If religion does not produce a more ethical, loving society, something is fundamentally wrong with the way religion is being practiced."

Ignorance of the Bible and failure to practice principles that the Bible teaches are obvious from the results of this poll. The world is desperately looking for workable guidelines, and the Bible offers the only ones that are absolutely dependable. It is our handbook for survival, but in all too many Christian homes it is unknown and unused, and in too many churches it is not taught or preached.

Ignorance is not bliss; it can bring death. In July of 1876 the body of General George Armstrong Custer was found naked, reclining against the carcass of a horse, and surrounded by the remains of his unfortunate command. He and his men had not known that they were going out against an Indian force that was the largest ever assembled on the Plains. Had he not been ignorant of this fact and acted accordingly, he and his regiment would have survived.

The Church as a whole is not as knowledgeable about the Bible as it should be. The Church as a whole is also in trouble. When nearly two-thirds of your membership does not show up for weekly meetings, your organization is in trouble. According to *Yearbook of American Churches*, 37% is the average attendance at worship services for the Church in America. When the members fail to support church programs, this may be seen as another sign of trouble. Statistics compiled by the National Council of Churches show that average church giving amounts to about 37¢ per member per week. (That is less than the price of a cup of coffee.) When church membership increases at the rate of .03% per year (*Yearbook of American Churches*), this can hardly be considered evidence of successful outreach.

The churches that preach and teach the Bible are the ones that are growing. It is these churches that have something to offer in the way of guidelines and hope for a troubled world. God's statement that His Word would not return to Him void is the absolute truth. Martin Luther described the Bible as the manger in which we find Christ. Kierkegaard referred to it as God's Love Letter, and as we mentioned before, Emil Brunner likened it to the old phonograph ad that used the words, "His Master's Voice." All of these are good descriptions of the Bible, yet it is all these things and much, much more.

It instructs, comforts, exhorts, and inspires those who read and study it allowing the Holy Spirit to direct and enlighten them. God speaks to His people through His Word. The people in churches who feel that they can't get anything from reading the Bible are something like the boy who said he had never read *The Hunchback of Notre Dame* because he didn't keep up with college football. Both are dismissing something out of ignorance. The Bible, too often, has not been tried and found wanting; it simply has not been tried. It is imperative that the second mark of a healthy parish be that the Bible is given its rightful place as God's Word, His manual for living.

3. *The members are open to the empowerment and guidance of the Holy Spirit.*

The Holy Spirit is the promised Counselor, strengthener, and empowerer whom Jesus told His disciples to wait for. So it follows that churches exhibiting the first two marks of a healthy parish are open to the Spirit and all His gifts. The Holy Spirit always points us to Jesus, who always points us to the Father. The concept of God, the Three in One, is difficult to understand, and our understanding is certainly not helped when denominations get into theological arguments over the Trinity.

"You will know them by their fruits" is a good way to describe churches that are open to the Holy Spirit. They exhibit His gifts and manifest the fruit of the Spirit. Friendly warmth, love, and joy are apparent to even the casual visitor. They are concerned with the spiritual and physical welfare of the members, and have a strong missionary spirit. They take seriously Jesus' commands to die to self and reach out to others.

Such churches place a strong emphasis on prayer. They recognize that they are not self-sufficient, and they turn to the Lord often in prayer for guidance about specific problems as well as for strength to obey the guidance. Many of these churches have intercessory prayer groups whose sole function is to pray for the church, its members, and for such needs as may arise.

Forms of worship differ among them, but churches open to the Holy Spirit have a common theme in their worship:

that of praise. They understand that praise is the most important part of prayer, and whether they say so or not, they have discovered that God inhabits the praises of His people. As they join in singing songs of praise, they feel the Lord's presence in tangible ways. It is not unusual for the members to receive direct guidance on specific problems they have prayed about. In some of these churches this is called prophecy, in others, "a word from the Lord," while still others may simply say, "I feel that I got an answer to our problem." The semantics are not as important as the fact that God is communicating with His people and they are hearing and responding to Him.

An important function of the Holy Spirit is to sanctify or make holy. Members of churches that are open to the Holy Spirit are aware of their need for renewal and are open to being changed. Such churches are never satisfied with the status quo. They seem to have a restless energy and a sense of urgency that keeps things stirred up—moving and growing. These churches are a lot more fun and exciting than the more staid "man-directed" ones. John V. Taylor, in *The Go-Between God*, explains that it is not in our greater goodness but in our openness to one another in Christ's name that the Spirit possesses us. Our defenses must be down, broken by either intense joy or by despair, so that we have come to the end of ourselves. This is the prerequisite for renewal by the Holy Spirit.

4. *The church is a family.*

The members are bound together in a common love for God that gives them a genuine concern for each other. If you have problems they will pray with you, cry with you, and do anything they can to help solve them. If you have something to celebrate, they will rejoice with you. Their loving concern is expressed in a variety of ways. There is an ongoing effort to get to know one another and to include newcomers in the life of the parish. Members of such churches usually enjoy being together, and the church provides any number of activities to make this possible. Bible studies and other study groups, fellowship groups, prayer and praise meetings, impromptu meals together, and regularly scheduled covered-dish meals are just a few of the things that encourage the members to share time together.

There may be a committee that oversees help for families that are experiencing illness, a death, or a new baby, and need special attention. Every age group is considered important, from the infants to the oldest member. As a practical expression of this, such churches provide baby-sitting services for their activities and the grandmothers and grandfathers often volunteer their help. Because the members are open with each other and share their problems, as well as their joys, there is an awareness of needs as they occur. If a member loses a job, others may contribute to a help fund, if it is needed, and personal concern is given to help the person find work.

Weddings of members are celebrated as joyful occasions by the entire congregation, and at funerals the church family gathers to comfort and support the mourners. As in all families there may be a few strange cousins, but the rest accept them as part of the package and many times simply feeling accepted has a healing effect on the "odd ones."

Perhaps the single word that best describes a church that is a family is caring. The people truly care for one another. They "know it if you are sick, and care when you die" is the way former Speaker of the House Sam Rayburn explained why he wanted to go home to Bonham, Texas. In a church that is a family, one doesn't have to get sick to realize that the people care. You can see it in their smiles, their actions, and their attitudes. For many people such churches are where they learn the meaning of "family."

5. *The laity knows that it is the Church.*

One of the good fruits of the present renewal movement

is that so many lay people are discovering that they are the Church and are called to minister and to carry out Christ's commission as much as their ministers or priests. In churches that exhibit this mark, the clergy and laity work together as a team and there is a breakdown of the old artificial walls between them. They try to discover and use the gifts and abilities they have, and the individual is not afraid to acknowledge the weaknesses or inabilities he or she may have. They have caught the vision that Paul describes as "the whole body, joined and knit together by every joint with which it is supplied, when each part is working properly, makes bodily growth and upbuilds itself in love" (Ephesians 4:16). In Spirit-filled, Spirit-led parishes, the laity and the clergy understand that the ministry and mission belong to the whole Body. I wrote in a previous book that the role of the minister is to celebrate the sacraments and to be coach and cheerleader to the congregation: "Yea, God! Go get 'em, laity!"

Because so much has been written in recent years about the decline of church membership and the failings of the Church, many people ask, "Can anything good come out of the Church?" It seems that the visible church, like the little town of Nazareth, doesn't look like a very likely spot to produce anything world-changing. St. Paul answers this question with these words: "But God chose what is foolish in the world to shame the wise. . . . God chose what is low and despised in the world, even things that are not, to bring to nothing things that are, so that no human being might boast in the presence of God. He is the source of your life in Christ Jesus, whom God made our wisdom, our righteousness and sanctification and redemption; therefore, as it is written, 'Let him who boasts, boast of the Lord' " (1 Corinthians 1:27–31).

It is a miracle beyond understanding that almighty God should choose to use men and women to carry out His plan of salvation for the world. He has chosen to bestow on us the honor of becoming co-workers with Him in the ongoing creative process. We can recognize our weaknesses and our strengths as we allow God the Father, Son, and Holy Spirit to work in and through us. In all our personal weaknesses, He has given us His power and His authority to represent Him in and to the world. He can use "even things that are not, to bring to nothing things that are" (1 Corinthians 1:28). Even when we who are the Church are not what God calls us to be. He can use us to accomplish His purposes. All that is required of us is to say yes to Him, and then trust Him to use us as He will.

I have discovered that the Church can learn a great deal about working together as the people of God by observing Canada geese. These beautiful creatures seem to know inherently what we would do well to learn!

1. *When Canada geese fly in formation, they travel seventy percent faster than when they travel alone.*

This is an excellent example of why the Bible emphasizes so strongly the importance of unity. A unified group can attain goals—whether they be flying south for the winter or following Jesus as Lord—more easily and more quickly than can single units. The New Testament is filled with exhortations for unity. St. Paul, in particular, saw this need. His exhortations in Ephesians 1:10 and 4:3–4 are expanded in Philippians 2:2: "Complete my joy by being of the same mind, having the same love, being in full accord and of one mind."

Christians who have a common destination and travel in community move more quickly and easily than those who travel alone. Christians who try to keep their religion personal and private get sidetracked on their journeys and lose sight of the fact that Jesus Christ came to create a united community.

2. *The geese share leadership.*

The goose on the point of the inverted "V" formation is

in the most buffeted position. He catches the full force of the air currents and so tires more quickly than those who follow in more protected positions. When his energy is spent he rotates to the back and another goose flies forward to replace him. This is a good sermon on sharing leadership in a parish. Positions of leadership within the church catch the full force of the winds of criticism, complaints, and chores that are involved in maintaining the local church. They get tired; they get burned out! Everyone has occasional dry spells and needs to be refreshed and renewed. The twelfth chapter of 1 Corinthians reminds the Church that each member has talents and gifts that are to be used for the building up of the Body of Christ. Unless there is sharing and rotating of leadership, the gifts often go unused and the Church is poorer for it.

3. *Geese honk from behind to encourage those in front.*

The geese in the rear of the formation honk encouragement to those in the lead to keep up the speed. It is important to remember that there is a world of difference between squawking and honking! The geese seem to know by instinct something that we have to be taught: "Keep your tongue from evil, and your lips from speaking deceit" (Psalm 34:13); "If any one thinks he is religious, and does not bridle his tongue ... this man's religion is in vain" (James 1:26); "Let no evil talk come out of your mouths, but only such as is good for edifying, as fits the occasion, that it may impart grace to those who hear" (Ephesians 4:29). Encouragement is something everyone needs and something everyone can give.

4. *Geese keep company with the fallen.*

When a sick or injured goose drops out of the flight, at least one other goose joins him to help and protect him. Most churches will respond to the needs of physically ill members but often fail to reach out to those who have "fallen" for other reasons. Galatians 6:2 reminds us that it is in bearing one another's burdens that we fulfill the law of Christ, and 2 Corinthians 1:3-4 develops this theme more fully: "Blessed be the God and Father of our Lord Jesus Christ, the Father of mercies and God of all comfort, who comforts us in all our affliction, so that we may be able to comfort those who are in any affliction, with the comfort with which we ourselves are comforted by God."

We can learn from the geese that when one of our members drops away from the flock, somebody needs to check on him or her—and not necessarily the ordained minister. There is a story about a little girl who was late coming home from an errand. When her mother asked what took her so long, she replied, "Susie broke her doll and I had to help her." "How could you help her?" her mother asked. "I had to help her cry," was the answer. We in the Church often find when we check on a fallen member that the need is simply for someone to show love and sympathy as this little girl showed her friend.

Individually and corporately Christians have a high calling. We are called first to commit ourselves to Jesus as our Lord and Savior, then to unite with other believers as members of His Church, and to accept our ministry and mission in and to the world.

Jesus knew when He called the Christian Church into being that He was calling it to an awesome task, yet with the call came the promise to the fledgling Church that "the gates of hell shall not prevail against it" (Matthew 16:18, KJV). The Revised Standard Version of this reads: "The powers of death shall not prevail against it." Both translations are useful in understanding Jesus' mighty promise.

The reference to the gates of hell implies that Jesus knew that the Church would come under attack by Satan just as He Himself had. The wiles and designs of the devil haven't changed much since Jesus underwent the temptations in the wilderness. Satan's first attempt was to get Jesus to doubt

God's plan and activity. "If you are the Son of God. . . ." The other temptations were to abort the ministry that was set before Him, and to follow the devil instead of God. The Church continues to be subject to similar attacks as we are tempted to doubt the Church's mission and to settle for some lukewarm, pathetic imitation of our original high calling, and to abort the mission and ministry of being Christ's Body on earth.

"The powers of death" may seem more relevant to some of our churches today than "the gates of hell." There are so many "dead" churches that many people probably feel that the apathy or complacency that marks such churches is evidence that the devil has already won that battle. Not so! The proclamation of victory comes in the words *shall not prevail against it.* Jesus has equipped it with power and given it the authority to be His ministering Body on earth.

Therefore, Jesus' triumphant promise becomes our battle cry, as we move forward in the confidence that neither attacks from without or indifference from within the Body of Christ shall thwart God's purpose for His creation—the Church!